Liberty in Christ

by
John MacArthur, Jr.

MOODY PRESS
CHICAGO

© 1986 by
JOHN F. MACARTHUR, JR.

Library of Congress Cataloging-in-Publications Data

MacArthur John F.
  Liberty in Christ

  (John MacArthur's Bible studies)
  1. Freedom (Theology—Biblical teaching. 2. Bible.
N.T. Galatians V—Criticism, interpretation, etc.
I. Title. II. Series: MacArthur, John F. Bible studies.
BS2655.L5M33   1986   227'.406   85-29864
ISBN: 0-8024-5094-6 (pbk.)

1 2 3 4 5 6 7 Printing/GB/Year 90 89 88 87 86

Printed in the United States of America

Contents

CHAPTER   PAGE

1. Fallen from Grace—Part 1   1
   Tape GC 1665—Galatians 5:1-6

2. Fallen from Grace—Part 2   17
   Tape GC 1666—Galatians 5:7-12

3. What Is Christian Liberty?   33
   Tape GC 1667—Galatians 5:13-16

4. Walking by the Spirit—Part 1   49
   Tape GC 1668—Galatians 5:16-18

5. Walking by the Spirit—Part 2   65
   Tape GC 1669—Galatians 5:19-21

6. Walking by the Spirit—Part 3   81
   Tape GC 1670—Galatians 5:22-25

1
Fallen from Grace—Part 1

Outline

Introduction
A. The Empowerment of the Spirit
B. The Exhortation to Stand Firm
C. The Explanation of Freedom
   1. Escape
   2. Endowment
D. The Entanglement of Bondage

Lesson
I. The Work of False Doctrine
A. You Are Not Profited by Christ
   1. The dilemma
   2. The danger
B. You Are Required to Keep the Whole Law
   1. Stated
   2. Supported
     a) James 2:10
     b) Galatians 3:10
C. You Are Fallen from Grace
   1. The principle analyzed
   2. The principle applied
     a) To apostates
     b) To Christians
D. You Are Excluded from Righteousness
   1. The expectation of the future
     a) The promise of glorification
     b) The proof of grace
       (1) "Spirit"
       (2) "Wait"
       (3) "Faith"
   2. The effectiveness of faith
     a) The external shortcoming

b) The internal solution
   (1) Explained
   (2) Exemplified
   (3) Expressed
      (*a*) Galatians 5:14
      (*b*) Romans 13:8-9
      (*c*) Romans 8:4

Conclusion

Introduction

There are only two kinds of religion in the world: religion based on human achievement and religion based on divine grace. Although there appear to be, there aren't any others. Throughout history, God's religion of divine grace has been opposed by Satan's religion of human achievement or self-righteousness. The book of Galatians jumps into the middle of the controversy to resolve it. It capably defends the doctrine of divine grace over the doctrine of human achievement. For every man, salvation boils down to this simple question: Do I magnify my own achievements, or do I humbly bow beneath the grace of God? That is the issue facing every man.

A. The Empowerment of the Spirit

In Galatians 5 Paul emphasizes the ministry of the Holy Spirit because it is the Spirit who makes the life of faith work. A life of faith wouldn't work any better than a life of legalism if it weren't for the indwelling Holy Spirit who empowers us. Consequently, Paul calls us to yield to the Spirit's control through such statements as: "We through the Spirit wait for the hope of righteousness by faith" (v. 5); "Walk in the Spirit" (v. 16); "If ye be led by the Spirit, ye are not under the law" (v. 18); and, "If we live in the Spirit, let us also walk in the Spirit" (v. 25). It is necessary for those who have been justified by faith to implement a life of faith in the energy of the Holy Spirit.

B. The Exhortation to Stand Firm

Paul begins chapter 5 with a potent exhortation to the Galatians not to surrender the freedom that they have in Jesus Christ but to stand firm. They were set free from their pagan legalism when they believed in Christ. However, legalistic individuals known as Judaizers came along and tried to put them back into the bondage of legalism by requiring them to keep Jewish law. In verse 1 Paul says,

2

"Stand fast, therefore, in the liberty with which Christ hath made us free, and be not entangled again with the yoke of bondage." Paul told them that Christ set them free and that they were not to be in bondage again.

C. The Explanation of Freedom

1. Escape

Freedom, as expressed in Galatians, refers to freedom from the frustrating struggle to keep the law to gain God's favor. It is the freedom of knowing you are accepted by God because of what Christ has done. Such freedom is a tremendous kind of freedom, but it is more than just a deliverance from the oppression of legalism; it is also a positive endowment.

2. Endowment

Romans 6 and 7 picture a man without Christ as a slave to sin. But in chapter 8, he is set free. Whereas man could never please God by fulfilling God's law on his own, through the indwelling Holy Spirit man has the capacity to please Him. Freedom is not just a matter of being out from under the condemnation of the law; it also means being able to fulfill the law in the energy of the Holy Spirit.

From a positive standpoint, Paul views freedom as walking or living in the Spirit, which results in the production of spiritual fruit (Gal. 5:22-23), joy in doing the will of God (Rom. 15:32), and the fulfillment of the law of Christ (Gal. 6:2). Salvation gives us the freedom to obey the moral law out of internal power, not out of external constraint. The Spirit produces the ability in us to do what we could never do before we knew Christ. It is Christ who has made us free, not our own rituals or deeds. Galatians 3 says, "Christ hath redeemed us from the curse of the law, being made a curse for us" (v. 13). Christ paid a high price in sacrificing Himself to set us free. That sacrifice would have been pointless if Christ were to set us free only to put us in bondage again. There are some Christians who live in terrible legalistic bondage. That isn't freedom; that's just a transfer of bondage. You've been freed. Under the law a Jew had no more liberty than a child has under a guardian. A child is not old enough to act independently; therefore, he is always under restrictions and must be given orders. But once a

3

person comes to Christ, he becomes a mature son of God by faith (Gal. 3:25-26). At that point he is indwelt by the Holy Spirit (Gal. 4:6) and is a free man, no longer bound by external ceremonial restraints but able to exercise his liberty in the Spirit (Gal. 5:1). The Galatians had already been liberated from paganism, so there was no reason to put themselves under the ceremonial laws of Moses, which were no longer applicable under the New Covenant. In spite of that, they were on the verge of putting on the straitjacket of legalism.

When a person becomes a Christian, that doesn't mean he is free to be a criminal; it means he has the capacity to walk out of his cell and still live within the bounds of the law—not by being walled in, but by the internal restraints that are built in through the ministry of the Holy Spirit. Christian liberty is not being bound by rules but being free to obey God by walking in the Spirit. Galatians 5:16 says, "Walk in the Spirit, and ye shall not fulfill the lust of the flesh." In the Old Testament, the believers needed walls because the Spirit didn't permanently indwell believers. In the New Testament, believers can be controlled by the Spirit of God. The morality that God established hasn't changed. However, it can now be produced internally through the Holy Spirit.

D. The Entanglement of Bondage

The Galatians had acknowledged that salvation was by grace, through faith in Jesus Christ. The Holy Spirit was guiding them internally to change their behavior. But they wanted to turn around and walk back into the cell, thus confining the Holy Spirit to their cell. Paul warned them, "Christ set you free. Don't be entangled again with the yoke of bondage. He didn't go through all that trouble to turn you loose so you could go back into another cell. All you've done is stifle the Holy Spirit." The particular yoke of bondage that the Gentiles were being influenced to accept was the rite of circumcision. The Judaizers in Galatia were telling them they had to be circumcised to be fully accepted by God since they thought God accepted only those who had that sign of the covenant. Having escaped the ritualism of paganism, they were about to accept Jewish ritualism.

4

It is easier to live in a prison cell than it is to make right choices using your Spirit-directed freedoms. If you were in a cell, you would probably be a pretty good person. If you were walled in, there wouldn't be many things you could do. For example, the people of Israel while in the wilderness wanted to forget the Promised Land and return to Egypt. They felt it would be easier to be slaves in Egypt than to exercise their freedom. There are some people who are more comfortable when someone else lays down all the rules. They are not sensitive enough to the Holy Spirit to live apart from someone else's external guidelines.

The theme of Galatians 5 is that Christianity is freedom, not bondage. It's not freedom to do evil; it's freedom to do good by internal divine power, not external restraints. Paul makes his appeal in verse 1 and supports it in verses 2 to 12 by attacking the false doctrine of the Judaizers (vv. 2-6) and the Judaizers themselves (vv. 7-12). First he discusses the nature of the false doctrine, then he discusses the character of false teachers.

Lesson

I. THE WORK OF FALSE DOCTRINE (vv. 2-6)

The false doctrine that the Judaizers were teaching was salvation by good deeds. They believed Christians had to be circumcised to be accepted by God. You may ask, "Why did Paul make such a fuss over a minor surgical task?" He did it in the case of the Gentiles because false teachers were advocating circumcision as a necessary requirement for salvation. Although Paul tolerated that ceremonial ritual in the case of Timothy for maintaining an open channel of communication with Jewish people (Acts 16:3), he hated the system of works that it represented. The Judaizers were saying that faith in Christ was insufficient to redeem the Galatians. They believed Moses started the process of salvation, Christ continued it, but that it was up to the individual to finish it. That's legalism.

Paul suggests four consequences of abiding by the doctrine of salvation by works.

A. You Are Not Profited by Christ (v. 2)

"Behold, I, Paul, say unto you, that if ye be circumcised, Christ shall profit you nothing."

By using his name, Paul introduces this section with a strong

5

statement of apostolic authority. He may also be emphasizing his Jewishness, saying in effect, "Even I, a circumcised Jew, who is proud of his heritage and traditions, am telling you that circumcision is useless; it makes Christ of no benefit to you."

1. The dilemma

Beginning in verse 2, Paul puts his readers in a dilemma: You can choose circumcision or Christ but not both. A man's faith rests on Christ entirely or not at all. He presents a hypothetical situation in verses 2 to 4, set off with the word *if*. He is not talking to people who have been circumcised yet. Evidently, the Galatians already were following the Judaizers' advice to the extent that they were observing "days, and months, and times, and years" (Gal. 4:10). Many of them had already accepted the Judaistic calendar. But they had not yet gone beyond that.

2. The danger

The danger was that they would yield to circumcision and reduce their religion to a religion based on human achievement. If they accepted circumcision, thinking it was necessary for salvation, they would forfeit the benefits provided by Christ. Romans 11:6 says, "If [salvation is] by grace, then it is no more of works; otherwise grace is no more grace." If they added any works to grace—even if they were trusting 99 percent in Christ and only 1 percent in circumcision—they would be trusting in a system of works and not grace. Commentator William Hendricksen said, "A Christ supplemented is a Christ supplanted" (*New Testament Commentary, Galatians and Ephesians* [Grand Rapids: Baker, 1968] p. 195). Paul wanted to show that as far as justification is concerned, faith and works don't go together.

The Galatians had heard about Christ. Many of them had believed in Christ, and some of them were on the verge of believing. Accepting circumcision as part of their salvation would render Christ of no value to them. That is basic to the doctrine of salvation. It is impossible to receive Christ, acknowledging you can't save yourself, and then turn around and be circumcised, acknowledging that you *can* save yourself. You can't mix the two. You must choose between salvation by law and salvation by grace—between Christ and circumcision.

Salvation is through faith in Christ alone. Any person who believes that circumcision—or any other work, such as keeping the Sabbath or serving as a missionary—is necessary for salvation is showing that he disbelieves in the all-sufficiency of grace, and he will never be saved on his own merits. Christ's provision of salvation can't be worth anything if you don't fully trust Him.

The Galatians hadn't accepted circumcision yet, but many Jews were hung up on that ritual. In Romans 9 Paul draws a portrait of Israel struggling with legalism: "What shall we say then? That the Gentiles, who followed not after righteousness, have attained to righteousness, even the righteousness which is of faith" (v. 30). Although the Jews had been seeking righteousness, it was the Gentiles who found it in Christ. Verses 31-32 say, "Israel, who followed after the law of righteousness, hath not attained to the law of righteousness. Why? Because they sought it not by faith but, as it were, by the works of the law." Many Jews never found true righteousness because they were really searching for self-righteousness. But many Gentiles were invited to the banquet (cf. Matt. 8:11- 12).

So Paul says that the false doctrine of human achievement renders Christ's death worthless to you. His sacrifice on the cross would not profit you at all. His death would be meaningless if you counted on something you had done to save you. You would be ignoring the gracious work of Christ.

B. You Are Required to Keep the Whole Law (v. 3)

"I testify again to every many that is circumcised [lit., "who lets himself be circumcised"], that he is a debtor to do the whole law."

1. Stated

If you want to live by law, you must follow every law. The word "testify" (Gk., *marturomai*) should be translated "I protest" to adequately convey the intensity of Paul's statement. That Paul is protesting "again" may mean he is either repeating the warning of verse 2 or is repeating a warning he gave on a previous occasion. He makes it known that everyone who lets himself be circumcised is obligated to keep the whole law. If a person refuses to accept God's grace, the only other way he can be justified is by keeping the whole law—and that's impossible.

7

I accept the fact that God loves me and that He redeemed me by His pure grace. I didn't do one thing to add to my salvation. In fact, I'm scared to try to add to my salvation because then I'm required to keep the whole law. Those who try to keep the law on their own are in trouble because they can't.

2. Supported

   a) James 2:10—"For whosoever shall keep the whole law, and yet offend in one point, he is guilty of all." Can you imagine a Jew who had struggled all his life to keep the law to secure his salvation, yet broke one of the laws at the end of his life? What a horrible thing that would be. (Of course, realistically he never could have made it that far without breaking some of God's laws.)

   b) Galatians 3:10—"For as many as are the works of the law are under the curse; for it is written, Cursed is everyone that continueth not in all things which are written in the book of the law, to do them." Everyone under the law is cursed because no one can keep it completely. If you want to do good works to get to God, you are under a works system, and must make sure that you do nothing but good works. If you ever do anything else, you are cursed. If you want to trade in grace for that kind of a life, that's your privilege— and your biggest mistake.

So Paul warned that false doctrine renders Christ profitless and puts a person under the bondage of the entire legal system. You can't break one command and still expect to be saved by the law. Paul then gives the Galatians a third result of following the false doctrine of salvation by works.

C. You Are Fallen from Grace (v. 4)

"Christ is become of no effect unto you, whosoever of you are justified by the law; ye are fallen from grace."

1. The principle analyzed

Some people have read this verse and have panicked, because they believe the concept of falling from grace contradicts the doctrine of security, which simply states that a person can't lose his salvation. However, the passage here has nothing to do with the security of salvation. It is dealing with the contrast between law and

grace: If you include good works as part of the requirements for salvation, you have lost hold of grace and its
meaning. If a man believes in salvation by works, Christ
is rendered "of no effect." That phrase could be translated "severed from" (NASB*) or "cut off from" Christ. It
is similar to the statement at the close of verse 2. If a man
tries to combine law and grace as a means of salvation, he
makes Christ of no benefit because he puts himself under
the law. If he is going to live under the law alone, Christ
can't do anything for him.

2. The principle applied

   a) To apostates

   I don't think Paul was necessarily applying the concept of being severed from Christ to anyone in
   particular. He was just showing that law and grace
   don't mix as means of salvation. Being severed from
   Christ could apply to an apostate: someone who
   understands what Christ has done, but turns away,
   counting on his works to save him. He has fallen
   from grace into the pit of legalism.

   b) To Christians

   It is also possible to apply the concept of being
   severed from Christ to a Christian. You may ask,
   "Could a Christian fall from grace?" Yes, in a sense.
   You were saved by grace, and you are to live by
   grace—God's free favor on your behalf. God's blessing comes when you yield to the Spirit. When you
   operate in the flesh, you close the door to God's
   blessing. When a Christian lives in the flesh, he
   forfeits the blessing he would receive if he were living
   in the Spirit. Second Corinthians 9:8 says that "God is
   able to make all grace abound toward you." That's a
   tremendous promise. God's wants to unload bless-
   ings on us, but the condition is our Spirit-led service.
   In that particular passage it was the condition of
   Spirit-led giving. If the Corinthians responded to the
   Spirit in the matter of giving, God would pour His
   grace on them in return.

   A person can be saved and not grow in grace. Peter
   said, "Grow in grace" (2 Pet. 3:18), which implies not
   every Christian does that automatically. However,

New American Standard Bible

just because a Christian refuses the grace of sanctification does not mean he forfeits the grace of justification. If a Christian loses his grip on grace as a way of life, that doesn't mean God has lost His grip on him in terms of saving grace. The process of sanctification can be retarded by the flesh. A Christian can live in the flesh, hoping to earn God's favor, but that only cuts him off from the flow of daily blessing. If justifying grace were interrupted every time sanctifying grace was interrupted, it wouldn't be worth anything; you would need to retain your salvation by works. If every time you sinned you lost justifying grace, how would you keep it except by working for it? Salvation would no longer be the result of grace but of works. If you try to add works to grace, you destroy grace.

D. You Are Excluded from Righteousness (vv. 5-6)

If you try to live by law, you forfeit the righteousness you are looking for. Romans 9:30-32 says that the Jews sought to become righteous, but they missed out because they sought to attain that by the works demanded in the law.

1. The expectation of the future (v. 5)

"For we through the Spirit wait for the hope of righteousness by faith."

a) The promise of glorification

We accept righteousness not by works but by faith. Judaizers and any other adherents to the religion of human achievement are hoping to attain righteousness through their works. Paul contrasts them with Christians, who wait for righteousness through the Spirit by faith. Although righteousness is ours right now, there is an aspect of it that is hoped for. When we are ushered into the presence of Christ, "we shall be like him" (1 John 3:2). There will be a fullness of righteousness that will be ours when we see Jesus Christ face to face. Paul says in Romans 8, "For the earnest expectation of the creation waiteth for the manifestation of the sons of God. . . . The creation itself also shall be delivered from the bondage of corruption into the glorious liberty of the children of God" (vv. 19, 21). There is a future aspect of righteousness that we still wait for. Although we as

10

Christians presently possess the righteousness of Christ, which was imputed to us when we believed, there is a sense in which we are waiting for a greater fulfillment of that righteousness.

b) The proof of grace

Verse 5 has three words that seal the argument against earning righteousness.

(1) "Spirit"

Those who seek to attain righteousness by the law do so through their flesh, not through the Spirit. But the righteousness Christians hope for comes through the Spirit.

(2) "Wait"

The test doesn't say we're to work for righteousness; it says we're to wait for it. You may hear someone say, "I was saved and now I am working to be one of the 144,000 in Revelation 7." I'm not working for righteousness; I'm waiting to receive it. It will be as free a gift to me as my salvation was. When I die and go to be with the Lord, I will be made completely righteous. I do good works, but I don't work for righteousness. I work because my heart is filled with love for Christ. Such love issues in good deeds. I'm not trying to earn anything. My service is merely my response to what God has done for me.

(3) "Faith"

Glorification will be mine by faith, not by works. I wait in faith for that divine gift and God will respond by bestowing completed righteousness on me.

2. The effectiveness of faith (v. 6)

a) The external shortcoming (v. 6*a*)

"For in Jesus Christ neither circumcision availeth anything, nor uncircumcision".

Circumcision isn't even an issue in Christ. A Gentile boasting about his lack of circumcision or a Jew boasting about his circumcision as the sign of the covenant are both irrelevant. Only grace and faith matter.

The trouble the Corinthians were having illustrates that external rituals have no effect on a person's spirituality. When the Corinthians bought meat at the market place, it was likely that it had already been offered to idols. After people gave their meat offering to the priests, the priest would sell the meat in the market to make money. Christians who wanted to buy meat experienced an ethical struggle, wondering if the meat had been offered to idols. Paul reassured the Corinthian Christians that an idol is nothing (1 Cor. 8:4). He says, "But food commendeth us not to God; for neither, if we eat, are we the better; neither, if we eat not, are we the worse" (v. 8). Who cares whether we eat or don't eat? It doesn't make any difference. External rituals and ceremonies don't mean anything to a person who is in Christ.

b) The internal solution (v. 6b)

"But faith which worketh by love."

(1) Explained

If Paul hadn't added that last phrase, someone could complain, "You Christians just get saved, then you sit around and don't do anything!" Certainly we work. However, we don't work to gain righteousness; we work because of love. The whole law is fulfilled when faith works by love. Instead of working by external rules, I work out of love, which internally motivates me.

(2) Exemplified

For example, the law says, "Thou shalt not kill" (Ex. 20:13). Let's suppose I'm living under law without the indwelling Holy Spirit producing love in my life. If someone had done something to me and I decided to kill him, perhaps the only thing that would restrain me would be that external prohibition. But if I love that individual, I will not kill him. The law says, "Thou shalt not steal" (Ex. 20:15). But if I love people, I'm not going to steal from them. The power to do what's right is motivated internally, not externally. Devoted love, which springs from the Holy Spirit, operates in the life of faith and precludes the necessity of law.

(3) Expressed

    (a) Galatians 5:14—"For all the law is fulfilled in one word, even in this: Thou shalt love thy neighbor as thyself." If you love people, you aren't going to kill them, steal from them, covet their wives, or lie to them.

    (b) Romans 13:8-9—"Owe no man any thing, but to love one another; for he that loveth another hath fulfilled the law. For this, Thou shalt not commit adultery, Thou shalt not kill, Thou shalt not steal, Thou shalt not bear false witness, Thou shalt not covet; and if there be any other commandment, it is briefly comprehended in this saying, namely, Thou shalt love thy neighbor as thyself." Love is the fulfilling of the law. So instead of having to keep the law by external restraint, I can keep the law from the inside out, because the Spirit is producing love in me.

    (c) Romans 8:4—Paul knew Christ was crucified "that the righteousness of the law might be fulfilled in us, who walk not after the flesh, but after the Spirit" (v. 4). I fulfill the law by the Spirit dwelling within me. It could never be fulfilled by relying on externals.

So my faith produces works of love, but my working is not to obtain righteousness. I already have been declared righteous in Christ. My works are the result of His righteousness.

Conclusion

One who believes the false doctrine of salvation by works finds that Christ profits him nothing, he is debtor to the whole law, he is fallen from grace, and is excluded from righteousness—righteousness belongs only to those who come to God in faith. There was an artist who dreamed of sculpting a masterpiece of multiple characters. Finally receiving a commission from a donor to do a work that was to be placed in a museum, the artist began the work he was sure would bring him honor and fame. After he had spent a lifetime toiling at his masterpiece, it was finished and ready to win the acclaim of the world. Unfortunately, there was no way to get the massive sculpture out of the room he had built it in. His masterpiece was held captive in the room in which he had worked. That's a good illustration of a man trying to earn his way to heaven: Everything he does in this world to merit acclaim from God will be left in this world. There will never be any applause from God for acts of self-righteousness. Whatever you do to earn salvation by works will perish with this earth. Salvation is by grace through faith alone.

Focusing on the Facts

1. Identify the two basic kinds of religion (see p. 2).
2. What makes the life of faith work (see p. 2)?
3. From what had the Galatian Christians been set free by believing in Christ? To what would the Judaizers have put them in bondage (see p. 2)?
4. Explain the negative and positive aspects of a Christian's freedom (see p. 3).
5. What was the particular yoke of bondage that the Gentiles were being influenced to accept (see p. 4)?
6. Why did Paul tolerate circumcision in the case of Timothy but not in that of the Galatians (see p. 5)?
7. What is ironic about the search for righteousness according to Romans 9:30-32 (see p. 7)?
8. Why would it be necessary for the Galatians to keep the whole law if they chose to be circumcised? Support your answer with Scripture (see p. 7).
9. What does it mean for a Christian to be severed from Christ and fall from grace (see pp. 8-9)?
10. If a Christian lost justifying grace when he sinned, how would he be obligated to retain his salvation (see p. 10)?
11. What are Christians waiting for, according to verse 5 (see p. 10)?
12. What three words in verse 5 lend support to the fact that our righteousness is not earned by working for it? Explain the concepts behind them (see p. 11).
13. What did Paul assure the Corinthian Christians in 1 Corinthians 8 (see p. 12)?
14. Why do Christians do good works (see p. 12)?
15. How is the law fulfilled by Christians (see p. 13)?

Pondering the Principles

1. How disciplined are you as a Christian? Since you have been set free from your previous pattern of life, have you consistently depended upon the Holy Spirit to lead you in your life of freedom? Whereas a prisoner would have a very regimented life while in jail, he would have the freedom to do almost anything

he wanted when released. The question is: Would he use his freedom in a profitable way, or would he fall back into the self-destructive patterns that sent him to jail? As Christians, we should be using our freedom to nurture our spiritual growth and bring glory to God. How are you stimulating yourself spiritually on a daily basis? What are you doing to bring honor to the God who created you and saved you? Memorize 1 Corinthians 6:20 and Galatians 5:13 as you consider the answer to those questions.

2. Galatians 5:5 says Christians are waiting "for the hope of righteousness by faith." Although we were declared righteous when we believed in Christ, there is still a fuller righteousness that we will receive when we are glorified as we enter heaven. That fact ought to motivate us to live godly lives now. Read Colossians 3:1-17. Are you seeking "those things which are above" (v. 1)? Are your goals, plans, and activities structured around how they relate to Christ and His kingdom? Reevaluate your life. Determine if you are still on course, pressing "toward the mark for the prize of the high calling of God in Christ Jesus" (Phil. 3:14) or if you have wandered off course. Praise God for the grace by which He has saved, empowered, and preserved us for His glory as you meditate on Ephesians 2:1-10 and Romans 8:28-30.

2
Fallen from Grace—Part 2

Outline

Introduction

Review
I. The Work of False Doctrine

Lesson
II. The Work of False Teachers
   A. They Hinder the Truth
      1. The opponents of the truth
      2. The obedience to the truth
         a) Explained
            (1) Its reference to salvation
               (*a*) Acts 6:7
               (*b*) Romans 2:8
               (*c*) Romans 6:17
               (*d*) Romans 10:16
            (2) Its reference to sanctification
               (*a*) 2 Corinthians 10:4-5
               (*b*) Romans 6:16-18
               (*c*) 1 Peter 1:22
         b) Exemplified
            (1) 1 Timothy 4:1-2
            (2) 2 Timothy 3:8
            (3) 2 Peter 2:1-2
   B. They Are Not of God
   C. They Contaminate the Church
   D. They Will Be Judged
      1. The confidence
         a) John 8:31
         b) John 15:4-8
         c) Philippians 1:6
      2. The condemnation

      a) Matthew 23:33
      b) 2 Peter 2:1-14
      c) Matthew 18:1-6
  E. They Persecute True Teachers
    1. The defense of Paul's persecutions
      a) The accusation about Paul
        (1) Expressed
        (2) Explained
      b) The argument by Paul
    2. The denouncement of Paul's persecutors

Conclusion

Introduction

Paul was concerned about the Christians in Galatia because false doctrine had penetrated their churches. The Galatians had come out of paganism. They had forsaken heathen practices and had accepted the freedom of salvation that comes with belief in Christ. They were, in fact, converts of the apostle Paul himself, having received the Holy Spirit and manifested His fruit in their lives. Consequently, they had begun to make an impact on their community.

At a later date, the Judaizers arrived and told them it was not sufficient to believe in Christ alone for salvation. They were convincing the Galatians that it was necessary to obey the Mosaic ceremonial law. But that was nothing short of legalism—attempting to please God through works, rather than faith. Legalism is the belief that if you perform certain religious activities, God will save and bless you on that basis rather than on faith and the attitude of your heart. Salvation by works is precisely what Paul argues against in the epistle to the Galatians. Salvation is not a question of what you do; it's a question of what you believe. It is a question of faith, not works.

In the first two chapters of Galatians, Paul establishes his right to preach the message of salvation by faith rather than works. In chapters 3 and 4, he establishes that the Old Testament teaches salvation by faith and grace. Finally, in chapters 5 and 6, he demonstrates how to live out the freedom of salvation and revealed that the life of faith is blessed of God.

Review

Galatians 5:1 tells us that Christ set us free not to become bondslaves to a legal system, but to empower us to operate within God's moral law, which is still valid. In fact, Paul said, "The law is holy, and the commandment holy, and just, and good" (Rom. 7:12). But as a

18

Christian, I do not expect my ability to keep that law to save me. Salvation is a matter of faith and grace only. In Galatians Paul says that Christ has given us the freedom to walk in the Spirit to keep from fulfilling the lusts of the flesh. Being liberated doesn't mean a Christian can be free to sin whenever he wants and get away with it; it means he can overrule his compulsion to sin through the indwelling Holy Spirit. Christian liberty is being controlled from the inside, rather than being pressured from the outside. It is freedom to do what I want out of love, not bondage to do what I have to out of fear.

Paul exhorted the Galatians to continue to stand firm and not be oppressed by the yoke of legalism. In writing to them, he attacks both the false doctrine and the false teachers in verses 1 to 12.

I. THE WORK OF FALSE DOCTRINE (vv. 2-6; see p. 5)

True faith produces good works. The works themselves do not save a person. They are merely the result of being transformed through faith. Colossians 1:10 helps clarify how good works relate to salvation: "That ye might walk worthy of the Lord unto all pleasing, being fruitful in every good work." God desires a Christian to be fruitful and productive in good works. The works of a Christian's life do not earn him salvation or favor with God; rather they indicate that he has been saved. When we become new creations in Christ, the Holy Spirit produces good works. The law, however, has a problem: It can't change people on the inside. But the Spirit who lives within us gives us the capacity to keep God's law. The law may restrict behavior, but it never changes people. Salvation by grace through faith internally changes people.

After condemning the false doctrine of legalism, Paul condemns the false teachers themselves.

Lesson

II. THE WORK OF FALSE TEACHERS (vv. 7-12)

A. They Hinder the Truth (v. 7)

1. The opponents of the truth (v. 7a)

"Ye did run well; who did hinder you?"

Paul commends the Galatians for having run the race of the Christian life so well. But some Judaizers had put legalistic obstacles in the track and hindered the good start and the fruitful progress of the Galatian churches.

19

Therefore, Paul asked, "Who hindered you by moving in and draining you of your power?" More than wanting to identify the individual false teachers by name, he was making a statement of amazement: "I can't believe you could ever allow anyone to do a thing like that! Who could possibly discount my authority and claim to improve on the Spirit's work so that they could destroy what God began among you?"

The Galatians had believed God until legalism entered their churches and their members began to stumble. Paul did not ask them to name the ringleader. He said, "Before you continue to follow the false teaching of this group, you'd better consider what kind of persons they are." Paul wanted his readers to evaluate the character of false teachers.

Paul had this to say about the kind of people they were: "As many as desire to make a fair show in the flesh, they constrain you to be circumcised. . . . For neither they themselves who are circumcised keep the law, but desire to have you circumcised, that they may glory in your flesh" (Gal. 6:12-13). They only wanted converts to add to their list of accomplishments. That is typical of false teachers: they want to get a following of people who support their aberrant teachings.

2. The obedience to the truth (v. 7*b*)

    "That ye should not obey the truth?"

    a) Explained

    (1) Its reference to salvation

    Obeying the truth can refer to the truth of salvation. The Galatians may have actually begun to forsake the doctrine of salvation, coming to the place where they no longer believed the truth.

    (*a*) Acts 6:7—"The word of God increased, and the number of the disciples multiplied in Jerusalem greatly; and a great company of the priests were obedient to the faith." Many priests also believed in Christ, which resulted in their salvation.

    (*b*) Romans 2:8—To those who are "contentious, and do not obey the truth, but obey unrighteousness [will come] indignation and wrath." Those who reject salvation will experience divine judgment.

(c) Romans 6:17—"God be thanked, that whereas ye were the servants of sin, ye have obeyed from the heart that form of doctrine which was delivered you."

(d) Romans 10:16—"They have not all obeyed the gospel." The concept of obeying the truth often refers to salvation (cf. Rom. 15:18; 16:26; 2 Thess. 1:8).

(2) Its reference to sanctification

Obedience to the truth is not only an issue of salvation; it is also related to the Christian life. You may ask, "Is Paul talking to Christians or non-Christians in the fifth chapter of Galatians?" I think he is saying, "You started out right by obeying the truth of salvation and the truth of living in the Spirit, but someone is hindering you from being committed to those truths." The issue isn't whether he is talking to Christians or non-Christians; he is talking about principles that can apply in either case.

It is sad that a church founded by the apostle Paul was forsaking the doctrines of salvation and sanctification. Throughout the world, there are many churches that propagate falsehood regarding salvation, even though they may be part of the church. Sometimes Christians can find themselves falling into a pattern of legalism when they disregard the truths about the grace of God.

(a) 2 Corinthians 10:4-5—"(For the weapons of our warfare are not carnal, but mighty through God to the pulling down of strongholds), casting down imaginations, and every high thing that exalteth itself against the knowledge of God, and bringing into captivity every thought to the obedience of Christ." The believer is to be obedient to Christ's leading in his life.

(b) Romans 6:16-18—Paul wrote that if we have yielded ourselves as servants of Christ, we ought to obey Him.

> (c) 1 Peter 1:22—Peter talked to Christians about
> obeying the truth and loving the brothers.

Sometimes even well-meaning people can sell the church a bag of legalism—dos and don'ts that are supposed to be the equivalent of spirituality. When churches accept that, they are hindered from serving. When non-Christians on the edge of Christianity forsake the true doctrine of salvation, or when Christians exchange the truth of grace for legalism, the result is the same: The race toward spiritual maturity cannot be run in the shackles of legalism. There will be no fruitfulness when legalism is preached, because legalism prevents the listeners from applying the truths that edify them.

b) Exemplified

> (1) 1 Timothy 4:1-2—"Now the Spirit speaketh expressly that, in the latter times, some shall depart from the faith, giving heed to seducing spirits, and doctrines of demons, speaking lies in hypocrisy, having their conscience seared with a hot iron." False teachers typically fail to live by the message they preach, a hypocritical practice that doesn't seem to bother them since their consciences are insensitive to the power of conviction. Their consciences had been rendered insensitive by scar tissue that developed because of their repeated refusals to heed the warnings of conviction.

> (2) 2 Timothy 3:8—False teachers "resist the truth, [being] men of corrupt minds, reprobate concerning the faith."

> (3) 2 Peter 2:1-2—"There shall be false teachers among you, who secretly shall bring in destructive heresies, even denying the Lord that bought them. . . . And many shall follow their pernicious ways, by reason of whom the way of truth shall be evil spoken of." One common characteristic of apostates is that they deny the deity of Christ. Such teachers bring error and thereby hinder the truth.

B. They Are Not of God (v. 8)

"This persuasion cometh not of him that calleth you."

The Galatians were not led by the Spirit into legalism. After all, it was the Spirit of God who had called them into freedom. Romans 8:30 tells us that God calls people to salvation: "Moreover, whom he did predestinate, them he also called; and whom he called, them he also justified; and whom he justified, them he also glorified." So Paul says that persuasion to follow legalism did not come from God. The God who called them to salvation through His internal, effectual, saving call does not propagate that kind of message.

In 2 Thessalonians 2:13-14 Paul says, "But we are bound to give thanks always to God for you, brethren beloved of the Lord, because God hath from the beginning chosen you to salvation through sanctification of the Spirit and belief of the truth, unto which he called you by our gospel, to the obtaining of the glory of our Lord Jesus Christ." God's saving call is administered through a presentation of the gospel. Because the false teachers among the Galatian churches were propagating a different gospel, they were not aligned with God, who had called the Galatians through the true gospel. Whatever voice the Galatians were hearing, it wasn't God's voice.

C. They Contaminate the Church (v. 9)

"A little leaven leaveneth the whole lump."

That was a very familiar proverb of Paul's day. Paul also used it in 1 Corinthians 5:6. Leaven is yeast. Only a little is required to get a great result. Just as a little leaven causes the whole lump of dough to rise, so a few false teachers can contaminate an entire group of churches.

Jude 11-13 describes false teachers: "Woe unto them! For they have gone in the way of Cain [the religion of human achievement], and ran greedily after the error of Balaam for reward [as a prophet for hire], and perished in the gainsaying of Korah [who usurped the role of a priest]. These are spots in your love feasts, when they feast with you, feeding themselves without fear; clouds they are without water, carried about by winds; trees whose fruit withereth, without fruit, twice dead, plucked up by the roots; raging waves of the sea, foaming out their own shame; wandering stars, to whom is reserved the blackness of darkness forever." Jude was a picturesque writer. Just as it took only one worm to destroy Jonah's gourd (Jonah 4:7), or as cancer can spread from one small cell to the rest of the body, or even as one match can start a forest fire, so one false teacher can contam-

23

inate a church. Benjamin Franklin realized that something seemingly insignificant could have severe consequences when he said, "For want of a nail, the shoe was lost; for the want of a shoe the horse was lost; for want of a horse the rider was lost; for want of a rider the battle was lost; and for want of a battle the kingdom was lost. All this for want of a horseshoe nail" (a maxim prefixing *Poor Richard's Almanack*, 1758). If you give in just a little, you may be asking for trouble. Needless to say, the priority of the leaders in the church is to watch and warn against false teaching because it can contaminate the church so rapidly.

D. They Will Be Judged (v. 10)

1. The confidence (v. 10a)

"I have confidence in you through [or "in"] the Lord, that ye will be none otherwise minded."

Paul's hope was like a star glimmering in the dark night. He was saying, "If you Galatians are genuine believers, you will recognize your situation and remain faithful to the truth."

a) John 8:31—Jesus said, "If ye continue in my word, then are ye my disciples indeed."

b) John 15:4-8—True disciples are fruitful branches that abide in Christ.

c) Philippians 1:6—"He who hath begun a good work in you will perform it until the day of Jesus Christ."

Similarly, Paul told the Galatians, "If you belong to Christ, I'm not going to worry that you will reject the truth. Your current brush with legalism is a passing fancy. I have confidence that you will stay with grace." Paul knew if they were Christ's, Satan had no power over them. John 10:28-29 says that those who belong to Christ are hidden in His hand and the Father's hand; and no one is able to pluck them out.

2. The condemnation (v. 10b)

"But he that troubleth you shall bear his judgment, whosoever he be."

The false teachers who were troubling the Galatians would receive judgment. The word translated "troubleth" means "to throw into confusion." Paul was saying, "Whoever created this chaos and confusion is in trouble himself." Many verses speak of the condem-

24

nation that will come on those who mislead God's people.

a) Matthew 23:33—Jesus condemned the scribes and Pharisees, saying, "Ye serpents, ye generation of vipers, how can ye escape the damnation of hell?"

b) 2 Peter 2:1-14—"But there were false prophets also among the people, even as there shall be false teachers among you, who secretly shall bring in destructive heresies, even denying the Lord that bought them, and bring upon themselves swift destruction. . . . Whose judgment now for a long time lingereth not, and their destruction slumbereth not. For if God spared not the angels that sinned, but cast them down to hell, and delivered them into chains of darkness, to be reserved unto judgment; and spared not the old world, but saved Noah, the eighth person, a preacher of righteousness, bringing in the flood upon the world of the ungodly; and turning the cities of Sodom and Gomorrah into ashes, condemned them with an overthrow, making them an example unto those that after should live ungodly; and delivered just Lot, vexed with the filthy manner of life of the wicked, . . . the Lord knoweth how to deliver the godly out of temptations, and to reserve the unjust unto the day of judgment to be punished; but chiefly them that walk after the flesh in the lust of uncleanness, and despise government [or authority]. Presumptuous are they; self-willed, they are not afraid to speak evil of dignities [or angels]. Whereas angels, who are greater in power and might, bring not railing accusation against them before the Lord. But these, as natural brute beasts, made to be taken and destroyed, speak evil of the things that they understand not, and shall utterly perish in their own corruption, and shall receive the reward of unrighteousness, as they that count it pleasure to revel in the daytime. Spots they are and blemishes, reveling with their own deceivings while they feast with you; having eyes full of adultery and that cannot cease from sin." That description of false teachers indicates their certain judgment for having sought to mislead God's people—a most serious offense.

25

c) Matthew 18:1-6—"At the same time came the disciples unto Jesus, saying, Who is the greatest in the kingdom of heaven? And Jesus called a little child unto him, and set him in the midst of them, and said, Verily I say unto you, Except ye be converted, and become as little children, ye shall not enter into the kingdom of heaven. Whosoever, therefore, shall humble himself as this little child, the same is greatest in the kingdom of heaven. And whosoever shall receive one such little child in my name receiveth me. But whosoever shall offend one of these little ones who believe in me, it were better for him that a millstone were hanged about his neck, and that he were drowned in the depth of the sea." Jesus made it clear that you do not tamper with God's people without incurring judgment.

E. They Persecute True Teachers (vv. 11-12)

1. The defense of Paul's persecutions (v. 11)

"And I, brethren, if I yet preach circumcision, why do I yet suffer persecution? Then is the offense of the cross ceased."

a) The accusation about Paul

(1) Expressed

Verse 11 is difficult to interpret at first glance, but it becomes easier to understand when you identify what Paul had been accused of. Apparently, the Judaizers were saying, "We're not so offbeat. Did you know that Paul also preaches circumcision? That makes Paul one of us." For evidence, they probably referred to the incident recorded in Act 16: "Then came [Paul] to Derbe and Lystra; and, behold, a certain disciple was there, named Timothy, the son of a certain woman, who was a Jewess, and believed; but his father was a Greek. Timothy was well reported of by the brethren that were at Lystra and Iconium. Him would Paul have to go forth with him; and took and circumcised him because of the Jews who were in those quarters; for they all knew that his father was a Greek" (vv. 1-3).

(2) Explained

You might wonder why Paul had Timothy circumcised. He certainly didn't do it to save him. He did it because Timothy was half Jewish and half Gentile. Everyone knew his father was a Greek, so Paul must have assumed that if Timothy would follow the rite of circumcision, those who knew Timothy would see that he purposely and willingly identified with Judaism. That made him all the more able to reach into the Jewish community and be accepted. Paul did it for the expediency of the ministry, not for Timothy's salvation. Paul wanted him to be a more effective missionary to Jews since they were the first people he approached when entering a new town and preaching in the synagogues. Timothy's acceptance of the sign of Judaism—a tradition he had a right to since he was half Jewish—enabled him to dialogue with those who otherwise might have rejected him.

When Paul wrote to the Galatians, however, he was not talking to Jews but to Gentiles. For them to assume circumcision was necessary to be saved would have been to violate the doctrine of salvation. When there was no biblical principle involved, Paul allowed for many things. In 1 Corinthians 9 he says, "And unto the Jews I became as a Jew, that I might gain the Jews . . . to them that are without law, as without law . . . that I might gain them that are without law. . . . I am made all things to all men, that I might by all means save some" (vv. 20-22). Without compromising biblical principles, Paul would accommodate himself to the situation. But apparently the Judaizers had cited the circumcision of Timothy to support their claim that Paul advocated circumcision.

b) The argument by Paul

Paul's argument was very effective. He said, "If I'm really on their team, why are they persecuting me?" The Judaizers persecuted him throughout Asia Minor and later in Macedonia and Achaia. If Paul had actually been teaching salvation by circumcision rather than through the cross of Christ, they wouldn't have persecuted him because the cross was an offensive concept to those who believed that salvation was earned by works. The offense of the cross to the Jew was not just a crucified Messiah; it was also that the cross superseded the entire Mosaic economy. The Jews had spent all their lives trying to keep the law. But when Christ died on the cross, thereby fulfilling the law, Paul could say, "It is no longer necessary to observe the entire law. What you need to do is believe in Christ and His work on the cross." They couldn't believe that one act of history at the cross could replace the Mosaic law. The cross basically made the legal system extinct. Fourth-century church Father John Chrysostom said in his commentary on Galatians 5:11 that the cross was not as great a stumbling block to the Jews as was the failure to require obedience to the ancestral laws. The example he gave is that when the Jewish religious leaders attacked Stephen, they didn't condemn him for worshiping Christ, but for speaking against the law and the holy place (Acts 6:13).

Paul himself persecuted the church before he became a Christian because Christianity seemed to have little place for Mosaic law. In Galatians 1:13-14, he says, "For ye have heard of my manner of life in time past in the Jews' religion, how that beyond measure I persecuted the church of God, and wasted it; and profited in the Jews' religion above many my equals in mine own nation, being more exceedingly zealous of the traditions of my fathers." So the cross was an offense to them because it superseded the very system they refused to let go of.

Are You Offended by the Cross?

The cross has offended people throughout history for one basic reason: It obliterates all religions of human achievement and strips every man naked in his own sin. People don't like to face the fact that they are naked in sinfulness before God and without recourse. Peter stood before the Jewish leaders in Jerusalem, after he had been arrested for teaching about Jesus and the resurrection from the dead, and said, "Neither is there salvation in any other; for there is no other name under heaven given among men, whereby we must be saved" (Acts 4:12). There aren't many people who like the narrow way of salvation by grace because it destroys all human achievement. The cross is still unpopular because it unmasks sin and leaves no room for pride in thinking you can earn your way to heaven.

To preach Christ as the only way of salvation is to invite persecution because it declares every man a sinner. It's much less offensive to preach something like circumcision. You could tell a person, "You're a nice guy. If you'll just do thirteen more nice things, you will go to heaven." But if you tell a person that he is a sinner and condemned to hell, and that his good works mean nothing to God, expect him to take offense.

2. The denouncement of Paul's persecutors (v. 12)

"I would they even cut off who trouble you."

Paul closed his polemic on false doctrine and false teachers with one of the most shocking statements that ever came from his lips. He said, "I wish those people who are teaching circumcision would castrate themselves!" There is something about his statement I like: his passionate hatred of false teachers. He wasn't afraid to say what he needed to. Bordering Galatia was the territory of Phrygia, where the goddess Cybele was worshiped. It was the practice of the priests and devout worshipers of Cybele to be castrated. All the priests of Cybele were eunuchs. So Paul said, "If you're going to go the route of human achievement and get yourself circumcised, you might as well go the whole route and castrate yourselves and become a full-fledged pagan!" Law and grace as means of salvation don't mix.

In the Christian sphere, some people might say, "It's nice to believe in Jesus Christ to be saved, but you must also add baptism to that." No, if you're going to add baptism, you might as well become a pagan. When the Galatians read verse 12 of Paul's epistle, they were probably shocked because they lived next to the Phrygians and knew exactly what he was talking about.

Conclusion

There are only two choices: the religion of divine grace or the religion of human achievement. Luke 18 illustrates them very graphically: "And [Jesus] spoke this parable unto certain who trusted in themselves that they were righteous, and despised others: Two men went up into the temple to pray; the one a Pharisee, and the other a tax collector" (vv. 9-10). The holiest people in the thinking of many Jewish people were the Pharisees, and the most despicable persons were tax collectors, who were the puppets of the hated Roman government. "The Pharisee stood and prayed thus with himself, God, I thank thee that I am not as other men are, extortioners, unjust, adulterers, or even as this tax collector. I fast twice a week; I give tithes of all that I possess" (vv. 11-12). When we love to talk about our religious accomplishments, we border on Pharisaism. If we brag about our praying, our giving, or our ministry, we are practicing the religion of human achievement. I don't know why this Pharisee even bothered praying to God; all he wanted to do was report in about how good he had been. However, the tax collector recognized his need of divine grace and therefore received it: "And the tax collector, standing afar off, would not lift up so much as his eyes unto heaven, but smote upon his breast, saying, God be merciful to me a sinner. [Jesus said,] I tell you, this man went down to his house justified rather than the other; for everyone that exalteth himself shall be abased; and he that humbleth himself shall be exalted" (vv. 13-14). The message of Galatians is very simple: Apart from the grace of God, there is no other means of salvation. No man ever comes to God on his own merit. God's arms are open; He graciously offers salvation to those who will believe in Him.

Focusing on the Facts

1. Explain what had happened among the Galatian churches that was concerning Paul (see p. 18).
2. What is legalism (see p. 18)?
3. Explain how good works relate to the Christian life (see p. 19).
4. What had the Judaizers done to the Galatian Christians (see p. 19)?
5. What two things can the phrase "obey the truth" (Gal. 5:7) refer to (see pp. 20-21)?
6. What happens when Christians exchange the truth of grace for legalism (see p. 22)?
7. According to 1 Timothy 4:1-2, what do false teachers typically fail to do? Why does that not seem to bother them (see p. 22)?

8. What is one reason the "way of truth" (Christianity) is spoken evil of, according to 2 Peter 2:1-2 (see p. 22)?
9. Who calls believers to salvation, according to 2 Thessalonians 2:13-14? What is the saving call administered through (see p. 23)?
10. How do we know the false teachers among the Galatians were not aligned with God (see p. 23)?
11. Explain how the proverb about leaven applied to the false teachers. Consequently, what is a priority for church leaders (see p. 23)?
12. Why was Paul confident about the Galatians (v. 10; see p. 24)?
13. What is promised to false teachers who mislead God's people (see pp. 24-25)?
14. What had the false teachers apparently accused Paul of that made it necessary for Paul to defend himself in verse 11 (see p. 26)?
15. Why did Paul circumcise Timothy in Acts 16? For what reason did Paul identify with others, according to 1 Corinthians 9:22 (see p. 27)?
16. What proved that Paul was not teaching salvation by circumcision like the Judaizers (see pp. 27-28)?
17. Why was the cross an offense to the Jewish person in general? Give two reasons (see p. 28).
18. Why do most people not like the narrow way of salvation by grace? Why is the cross still unpopular (see pp. 28-29)?
19. In the parable Jesus told in Luke 18, for what differing reasons did the Pharisee and the tax collector pray to God (see p. 30)?

Pondering the Principles

1. It is important that Christians prepare themselves against being misled by false teachings. Read Ephesians 4:11-14. What has Christ given to His church to mature each member? What is the goal of that edifying process? What is the result of having unity of faith and knowledge of the Son of God? Is your church offering a steady diet of biblical doctrine? It is said that a bank teller learns to detect counterfeit money not by studying the counterfeits but by being thoroughly familiar with the real thing. Do you know enough biblical truth to detect false or inaccurate teaching when you hear or see it? Besides examining the teachings themselves, evaluate the teachers who propagate them. What advice does Jesus give us about the relationship between a teacher's life and his doctrine, according to Matthew 7:15-20? How might you help the members of your church to equip themselves against false teachers?
2. When comparing Paul's readiness to become all things to all men

(1 Cor. 9:20-22) and his unwavering ministry of preaching the cross of Christ in the midst of opposition (1 Cor. 1:18— 2:5), there is a paradox: In his desire to win people to Christ, how could Paul identify with unbelievers, yet refuse to compromise the message of the cross even when it brought persecution? The issue is knowing what things can be compromised and what can't. Paul recognized that he could relate acceptably to unbelievers by accommodating himself to their various cultures. For example, if the situation called for it, he temporarily followed the ceremonial practices of the Jewish people, even though they were no longer binding (Acts 16:1-3; 18:18; 21:20-26). However, he never set aside the central truth of salvation by faith in Christ's death and resurrection. Examine Paul's sermon on Mars' Hill in Acts 17:22-34. He began dialoging at the level of understanding the Athenians had. Although he began in general terms, he didn't hedge when it came to telling them that God would judge the world through Christ, whom He raised from the dead (v. 31). Think of some people you know who need to hear the gospel. List some specific ways you might be able to identify with each of them to build a friendship. Before sharing Christ with them, think through ways you could make the gospel relevant to them.

3
What Is Christian Liberty?

Outline

Introduction

Lesson
I. What Christian Liberty Is
   A. The Release from the Obligation of the Ceremonial Law
   B. The Responsibility of Obedience to the Moral Law
      1. Explained
      2. Exemplified
II. What Christian Liberty Is Not
   A. Indulging the Flesh
      1. Its proponents
         a) 2 Peter 2:18-19
         b) Jude 4
      2. Its prevention
   B. Injuring Others
      1. The command to be considerate to one another
         a) Stated
         b) Supported
            (1) The context
            (2) The commands
               (a) Don't condemn others
               (b) Don't cause others to stumble
            (3) The conclusion
               (a) Evaluating what is important
               (b) Edifying those who are weak
      2. The consequence of consuming one another
   C. Ignoring the Law
III. How Christian Liberty Is Expressed

Introduction
We live in an age when men, women, and even children are seeking

33

liberation. "Do your own thing" is the manifesto of the freedom movement. Authority is being challenged as the individual follows the desire of his own heart. Self-centeredness is the motivating factor of worldly freedom. But that is not real freedom according to the Bible. Jesus says in John 8:34, "Whosoever committeth sin is the servant of sin." Although the liberation movements can't really set a person free, Jesus can. He said, "If the Son, therefore, shall make you free, ye shall be free indeed" (John 8:36). Freedom comes in Jesus Christ. That is the manifesto of Christianity. One reason it is difficult for Christians to understand current liberation movements is that they can't relate to bondage because of their liberty in Christ.

It is important to define our liberty in Christ because that phrase has been misused and misunderstood. When I say as a Christian that I am free in Christ, what do I mean? What is Christian liberty? What does it involve and how does it operate?

Lesson

I. WHAT CHRISTIAN LIBERTY IS (v. 13a)

"For, brethren, ye have been called unto liberty."

A. The Release from the Obligation of the Ceremonial Law

Galatians 5:1 says, "Stand fast, therefore, in the liberty with which Christ hath made us free, and be not entangled again with the yoke of bondage." Christ set us free to experience true freedom. Christian freedom is freedom of conscience, freedom from a legal system that couldn't be kept. It is freedom from the depressing awareness that we can't measure up to God. Christians do measure up in Christ. We have been "accepted in the Beloved" (Eph. 1:6).

The Galatian Christians had been adopted as sons of God, indwelt by the Holy Spirit, and freed from external ceremonial law. They were free in the Spirit to act out their own maturity and liberty from within. That was Paul's theme. Christianity is not slavery to a religious system; it is absolute freedom. Through Jesus Christ we have been delivered from the tiring, relentless performance of religious ritual. The Old Covenant law was external. It was given to demonstrate what true holiness is and to show men that they couldn't make it. The ceremonial practices were symbolic lessons that taught that sacrifice was necessary for sin. They pictured the final sacrifice of Christ. Once the reality came, there was no longer any need for the symbols.

Christian liberty is being free from having to fulfill the legal code to please God and free from the frustration of not being able to keep an external set of rules. In a positive sense, it is the freedom to function by the internal working of the Spirit. Because Christian liberty begins with faith in Jesus Christ, Paul tells the Galatians not to put their faith in circumcision or any other type of ceremonialism. According to Galatians 4:10, they had regressed from their freedom to observing "days, and months, and times, and years." For that reason Paul said, "I am afraid [for] you, lest I have bestowed upon you labor in vain" (v. 11). They were trying to accept Jewish rituals that no longer had any value.

B. The Responsibility of Obedience to the Moral Law

   1. Explained

      It is important to understand that the moral law of God hasn't changed—nor has the believer's obligation to it. The moral law is still binding. The doctrine of freedom was difficult for the Jewish people to accept. Because the teaching of Christian liberty posed a threat to their religious system, some of the Jews accused Paul of being antinomian. They assumed Paul was teaching that Christians had the liberty to do anything they wanted. The Judaizers who were misleading the Galatians charged Paul with rejecting God's ethical law. But Paul hadn't done that at all. He simply said that God's ethical law had become internal since Christ had come to live inside the believer.

      From the Old Covenant and the Mosaic law to the New Covenant and the law of Christ, the moral law has not changed in the mind of God. God has the same morality now that He had then. The difference is that Christians live under the internal restraints of the indwelling presence of the Holy Spirit. We are not reacting to a code. We are responding to a Person. The law was not set aside in its moral sense, but only in its ceremonial sense. Acts 10:9-15 supports that. The Lord said to Peter that it was now lawful to eat anything.

      The ceremonial law had two functions: to make Israel a unique nation (the Israelites had to live like no one else did), and to picture the coming sacrifice of the Messiah. Once the sacrifice of the Messiah was made, the pictures weren't needed anymore. Once the church was established, there was no longer a need to maintain Israel as a unique nation, for Jew and Gentile became one in Christ (Eph. 2:14). Although the ceremonial law was set aside, the moral law has not changed. In fact, through the Holy Spirit in your life, God will be able to accomplish what He endeavored to accomplish in the Mosaic law of the Old Testament. Christianity is not against the moral law of God.

The Dangers of Legalism and Libertinism

Let me illustrate how Christianity relates to the extremes of legalism and libertinism: Christianity resembles a narrow bridge spanning two streams. One of those streams is crystal clear but contains treacherous and deadly rapids; it symbolizes legalism— it appears to be a source of righteousness, but you can't stay afloat in it. Legalism will smash you on its rocks. The other stream is polluted libertinism—if you fall into it, you will drown because of its filth. Therefore, the Christian must maintain his balance on the bridge between the treachery of legalism and the filth of libertinism. Christians who have fallen into the rapids of legalism destroy the effectiveness of their spiritual lives. Those who are wallowing in the vices of libertinism put themselves in line for divine discipline. Galatians 5:13-16 tells us how to stay on the bridge.

Since we are no longer under the bondage of a ceremonial system, there is no reason to get circumcised or to observe feasts, new moons, and sabbaths. There are some people today who want all kinds of rituals. But there is no need for that. However, just because the ceremonial law is set aside does not mean that we change our morality. It doesn't mean that what God held as true in the Old Testament fades away with the coming of the New Testament. There is no change in the content of God's moral law, only a change in the way God brings about the fulfillment of it: from the external requirement of ceremonial law to the internal leading of the Holy Spirit.

2. Exemplified

Exodus 21 contains various instructions connected to the Ten Commandments, which are given in chapter 20: "Now these are the ordinances which thou [Moses] shalt set before them [the Israelites]. If thou buy an Hebrew servant, six years he shall serve; and in the seventh he shall go out free for nothing. If he came in by himself, he shall go out by himself; if he was married, then his wife shall go out with him. If his master have given him a wife, and she have borne him sons or daughters; the wife and her children shall be her master's, and he shall go out by himself. And if the servant shall plainly say, I love my master, my wife, and my children, I will not go out free; then his master shall bring him unto the judges. He shall also bring him to the door, or unto the door post; and his master shall bore his ear through with an awl, and he shall serve him forever" (vv. 1-6). A man could serve for six years under bondage because the law required it. However, he could walk out a free man on the seventh year. He could then use his freedom to serve his master because he loved him. There isn't one bit of difference in what the servant did the first six years and what he does the rest of his life. The only difference is that it has ceased to be an external requirement and has become an internal desire.

In the same sense, when a Jew came to Christ, he continued to serve God by obeying His moral code. However, he began to obey it not because it was required of him, but because he loved his Master and had the energy of the indwelling Christ to fulfill it. A devout Jew living by the moral and ceremonial codes of Moses would drop the ceremonies when he believed in Christ, but would retain the unchanging code of moral truth in the Old Testament. Only the reason for his behavior would change. He was freed from the law that exposed his sin. However, he was freed not to disobey, but to do what is right. The Christian doesn't need the external ceremonial laws anymore because the Holy Spirit restrains him from doing what is wrong and guides him to do what is right.

II. WHAT CHRISTIAN LIBERTY IS NOT (vv. 13b-15)

A. Indulging the Flesh (v. 13b)

"Only use not liberty for an occasion to the flesh."

Christian freedom is not an opportunity to indulge the flesh. In the New Testament the flesh is our fallen human nature, the part of us that is prone to sin. It is "the old man" (Col. 3:9). A Christian isn't set free in Christ to do whatever he wants. Some people wrongly think that because of the eternal security of the believer, they are free to do anything

37

they want. Christian liberty is *not* liberty to indulge the flesh. If you're saved, you won't indulge your flesh because of the sin-restraining presence of the Holy Spirit inside you.

Verse 13 tells us that we are not to use our "liberty for an occasion to the flesh." The word translated "occasion" (Gk., *aphormē*) is a military term referring to a base of operations. Don't make your flesh the base of your operation. Don't say, "I'm a Christian who's going to go to heaven; I can do what I want to do." You are not free to use your liberty as a springboard for the flesh. Paul denied the Judaizers' claim that he was teaching libertinism.

There are Christians on the borderline of believing the heresy that they can sin and get away with it without being condemned. They think they have the privilege of doing whatever they want and would say you can indulge in such things as booze, sex, or pornography by appealing to Christian liberty. It's very clear in verse 13 that Christian liberty is *not* to be used as an occasion for the flesh. In fact, I would seriously doubt the salvation of anyone who believes otherwise, because if he is saved, the Spirit will be restraining his sinful desires. Romans 8:9-11 tells us that one of the works of the Holy Spirit is to subdue the flesh.

1. Its proponents

   Whenever you hear someone propagating that Christian liberty allows for indulging the flesh, you can classify him as a false teacher.

   a) 2 Peter 2:18-19—Peter describes the character and promises of false teachers: "For when they speak great swelling words of vanity, they allure through the lusts of the flesh, through much wantonness, those that are just escaping from them who live in error. While they promise them liberty, they themselves are the servants of corruption; for of whom a man is overcome, of the same is he brought in bondage." Some people come to the place in life where they are seeking God or at least are sick of a sinful life-style. But if a false teacher comes along and tells them, "We've got the religion that says you can do what you want," they may put off their moral reform and be driven back down to the depths of sin.

   b) Jude 4—"There are certain men crept in unawares, who were before of old ordained to this condemnation, ungodly men, turning the grace of our God into lasciviousness [licentiousness]," Christian freedom is not freedom to sin; it's freedom from the power of sin.

2. Its prevention

The greatest liberty in the world is to be free from self-centered indulgence and able to serve God. The best example of that is Jesus. Romans 13:14 says, "Put ye on the Lord Jesus Christ, and make not provision for the flesh, to fulfill its lusts." Notice the contrast there: You either make provision for the flesh or you put on Jesus Christ. Jesus made no provision for His own desires. Paul said this of Him in Romans 15:3: "For even Christ pleased not himself." In John 4:34, Jesus says, "My food is to do the will of him that sent me, and to finish his work." Christ didn't please Himself. True Christian freedom is to be free from slavery to self desire and free to do whatever God wants you to do. That's an exciting kind of liberty. The implication is simple: our aim is not to please ourselves, but the Lord. Our motivation is not the stiff upper lip of duty; it's the loving service of gratitude to One who has set us free.

In the Old Testament, the area of sex is clearly defined. God tolerated no extramarital or premarital sex. There were severe consequences for anyone who engaged in adultery, fornication, bestiality, or homosexuality. Are we to presume that God changed His moral standards in the New Testament and we can now do whatever we want as long as we claim we love each other? For example, there are now churches for homosexuals. God hasn't thrown out Old Testament morality—God's standards haven't changed any more than God has changed. Hebrews 13:8 says, "Jesus Christ [is] the same yesterday, and today, and forever." Advocates of free sex have infiltrated Christianity. It's taken for granted that sexual love is the most important aspect of a relationship between any two people who love each other. A Christian is not free to abuse sex. The sexual freedom talked about today is the same slavery to self and lust of the flesh.

B. Injuring Others (vv. 13c, 15)

1. The command to be considerate to one another (v. 13c)

"But by love serve one another."

39

a) Stated

Someone could say, "I'm free in Christ so I'm going to do what I want," and then recklessly stomp upon other Christians. But this verse brings up the area of Christian liberty in relationship to my brother in Christ. My liberation is not a license to hurt my Christian brother but a freedom to serve him by a supreme kind of love (Gk., *agapē*). Such love requires that one set aside his personal ambitions and be willing to express his freedom in helping his fellow Christians. The word *serve* (Gk., *douleuō*) refers to the service rendered by a bondslave. It means to serve another Christian as his slave. Liberty and slavery in the Christian life form a paradox but not a contradiction, because such service is voluntary.

b) Supported

It's very easy for the Christian to use his liberty without regard for other believers. In Romans 14-15, Paul emphasizes the importance of service over selfishness.

(1) The context

Romans 14:1 says, "Him that is weak in the faith receive ye, but not to doubtful disputations." This passage illustrates two kinds of Christians: the weak and the strong. The weak Christian is legalistic and unable to accept his liberty in Christ, while the strong Christian understands his liberty. In the church at Rome, for example, there were many Jewish believers. When they learned that their freedom in Christ meant they were no longer required to keep the ceremonial laws, they were shocked. A Jew couldn't abruptly lay aside those laws without being hindered by his conscience. If he was invited over to a Christian brother's home and was served pork chops, his conscience wouldn't let him eat them. His host, who was stronger spiritually, might wonder what was wrong as he ate his pork chops in front of his guest. The stronger Christian would be flaunting his liberty and in so doing would be wounding the conscience of his weaker guest, who would think less of his host. Rather, the host should refrain from eating the pork to prevent offending his weaker brother.

40

Verse 2 says, "For one believeth that he may eat all things: another, who is weak, eateth herbs." Some weaker Christians might have been vegetarians to avoid eating meat that had been offered to idols. The New Testament makes it clear that all foods can be "received with thanksgiving" (1 Tim. 4:4) and that the distinction between clean and unclean animals is no longer applicable (Acts 10:13-15). After meat had been offered to various Greco-Roman deities, it would often be sold to people in the marketplace. To some weak Christians that was a stumbling block.

(2) The commands

(a) Don't condemn others

Paul instructed the Romans, "Let not him that eateth despise him that eateth not; and let not him who eateth not judge him that eateth; for God hath received him" (v. 3). God accepts the weak and the strong (the vegetarians and the meat eaters). One shouldn't make a big issue over what a Christian does or doesn't eat. Paul is essentially saying to the spiritually strong in chapter 14, "The weak person just hasn't discovered the meaning of his freedom. He is still a legalist at heart. He still sees Christianity as a set of rules."

Many churches set up a code of rules and expect the members to follow it. Churches that do that are implying that the work of the Holy Spirit is inadequate to guide them. They are trying to reestablish an external code. Some people do not understand their liberty, so they live according to certain rituals and rules. If you are a stronger brother who is not hung up on such things, don't mock a weaker one. Receive him as a beloved brother. Don't use your freedom as an excuse to make an issue over neutral things. By neutral, I don't mean clear biblical commands about something like baptism or reading the Bible. It could be something insignificant in itself, like shopping on Sunday. If, in a

41

weaker Christian's mind, there is something wrong with shopping on the Lord's Day, I am not going to force him to go shopping. I will accept him at his level of spiritual understanding and refrain from going shopping myself to prevent his being offended.

Paul told the Romans to let the Lord deal with the validity of the weaker brother's belief: "Who art thou that judgest another man's servant? To his own master he standeth or falleth. . . . One man esteemeth one day above another; another esteemeth every day alike. Let every man be fully persuaded in his own mind" (vv. 4-5). If perhaps a Jewish convert to Christianity wants to keep the Sabbath for a while, that's all right; don't offend him. There's no sense in making an issue out of it. Verse 6 says, "He that regardeth the day, regardeth it unto the Lord; and he that regardeth not the day, to the Lord he doth not regard it. He that eateth, eateth to the Lord; for he giveth God thanks; and he that eateth not, to the Lord he eateth not, and giveth God thanks." If a Christian wants to keep the Sabbath or eat a certain food, thinking that it is the right thing to do, don't make an issue out of it since those things don't really matter. The Lord will evaluate each individual at the judgment seat (v. 10).

First Peter 2:16, giving us similar instruction, tells us that we should never use our "liberty for a cloak of maliciousness." Don't flaunt your freedom over someone who doesn't understand it. You are going to meet legalistic brothers who may think it is wrong to dress a certain way or do certain things on the Lord's Day. The best thing to do is avoid the controversy. Don't flaunt your liberty; take consideration for your weaker brother.

(b) Don't cause others to stumble

Paul cautioned the Romans saying, "Let us not, therefore, judge one another any more;

42

but judge this, rather: that no man put a stumbling block or an occasion to fall in his brother's way" (v. 13). Verse 21 takes that general principle and particularizes it: "It is good neither to eat meat, nor to drink wine, nor anything by which thy brother stumbleth, or is offended, or is made weak." Although few today would be offended by eating foods offered to idols, there are some people who might be offended by people who drink wine. One of the reasons I don't drink is that drinking will inevitably make someone stumble. Causing someone to stumble means halting the spiritual progress of a Christian by doing something in front of him that his conscience doesn't allow him to do. You can also offend him and jeopardize your testimony, causing him to think less of you as a Christian because you have failed to lovingly make consideration for his immaturity. If he has stumbled and become offended, he will probably be "made weak" by falling further back into legalism as he observes your careless use of liberty.

(3) The conclusion

    (a) Evaluating what is important

        Paul said, "I know, and am persuaded by the Lord Jesus, that there is nothing unclean of itself; but to him that esteemeth anything to be unclean, to him it is unclean. But if thy brother be grieved with thy food, now walkest thou not in love. Destroy not him with thy food, for whom Christ died" (vv. 14-15). Gradually bring a weaker Christian to the place where he understands "nothing is unclean of itself." Jesus loved him enough to die for him, so don't show a lack of love by exercising your liberty to the point that you destroy your testimony and cripple him, pushing him further into legalism. Paul continued, "The Kingdom of God is not food and drink, but righteousness, and peace, and joy in the Holy Spirit. . . . For food destroy not the work of God" (vv. 17, 20).

43

(b) Edifying those who are weak

Paul made a concluding exhortation, saying, "We, then, that are strong ought to bear the infirmities of the weak, and not to please ourselves. Let every one of us please his neighbor for his good to edification. For even Christ pleased not himself" (15:1-3). Christian liberty does not mean we are free to injure our brother by doing whatever we want. We are free to lovingly serve that brother. There are some things in the so-called "gray areas" that are not wrong but may appear to be wrong to some people. So I don't do those things, because I don't want to consciously offend my brother. To do so would be an abuse of the liberty God gave me.

2. The consequence of consuming one another (v. 15)

"But if ye bite and devour one another, take heed that ye be not consumed one of another."

If you exercise your liberty, inconsiderately stomping all over everyone else, the whole church will end up fighting itself. If everyone exercises his own liberty, the unity of the Body of Christ will be destroyed. You may fear that constantly worrying about what everyone thinks will change your entire pattern of life. That's true, but it's wonderful to live like that. The Bible instructs us to serve one another out of love rather than maliciously injuring one another's spiritual growth by abusing our liberty.

C. Ignoring the Law (v. 14)

"For all the law is fulfilled in one word, even in this: Thou shalt love thy neighbor as thyself."

A Christian shouldn't say, "I'm free in Christ; I'm going to ignore the whole law." Freedom in Christ isn't freedom to ignore the law; it's freedom to fulfill the law. For Paul, the moral law was still the expression of the will of God. In Romans 7:22, Paul says, "I delight in the law of God." But he realized that he was not externally bound by the concrete forms of Judaism. He possessed the internal form of the law: the love of Christ flowing out of his life, in which the whole law is fulfilled. Paul quotes Leviticus 19:18 in Galatians 5:14, emphasizing that the law is summarized in love and can now be fulfilled by the indwelling Christ. The moral requirements of God's law haven't changed; it's just that now the basis of operation has gone inside. Christian liberty doesn't involve ignoring God's moral law. It fulfills it from the inside by love.

Romans 13:9-10 repeats Paul's point: "For this, Thou shalt not commit adultery, Thou shalt not kill, Thou shalt not steal, Thou shalt not bear false witness, Thou shalt not covet; and if there be any other commandment, it is briefly comprehended in this saying, namely, Thou shalt love thy neighbor as thyself" (v. 9). If you love, you don't need those laws because you won't kill, covet, steal from, or commit adultery against someone you love. If love is being exercised, the rest of the law is automatically fulfilled.

You may say, "I'd surely like to have that love." You were already given it the moment you were saved. Romans 5:5 tells us that when we were saved "the love of God is shed abroad in our hearts by the Holy Spirit who is given unto us." When a Christian acts on the principle of love, he is fulfilling everything that the Mosaic law was intended to accomplish, but from an internal motivation. We are called to freedom in Christ, not to serve self anymore, but to serve God first and then to serve others.

Christian liberty is not freedom to indulge the flesh but the capacity to use self-control. It is not freedom to injure others but to love them by ministering to them. And Christian liberty is not freedom to ignore the law but to fulfill it. Notice that Christian liberty affects our relationship to self, others, and God. Freedom is to be expressed by the Christian through self-control, love of others, and obedience to God's law. You may say, "It's nice to say that about our liberty in Christ, but how does it operate?"

III. HOW CHRISTIAN LIBERTY IS EXPRESSED (v. 16)

"This I say then, Walk in the Spirit."

The operation of Christian liberty is not automatic. We must walk in the Spirit. Rather than being under the control of a legal system, the believer has the potential of being controlled by a Person: God the Holy Spirit. When God set the law aside at the cross, He knew what He was doing. He didn't leave the world without leaving behind a restrainer. God governed the world for over 2,500 years before the Mosaic law was given. He can govern the world after the law has been set aside just as well. You say, "What about the rules? How will we restrain sin?" You will

45

restrain sin by the indwelling presence of the Holy Spirit. I would chafe under a legal system. In fact, I spent the most carnal years of my Christian life in a legalistic Christian institution where externals were being substituted for the work of the Holy Spirit. Consequently, I ignored the work of the Holy Spirit and endeavored to live by externals. But God will fulfill His entire law in us as we walk in the Spirit.

Focusing on the Facts

1. What is the motivating factor of worldly freedom (see p. 34)?
2. Why was the Old Covenant law given (see p. 34)?
3. What did the ceremonial practices teach and picture? Why were the symbols no longer needed with Christianity (see p. 34)?
4. Is the moral law still binding on Christians? Explain (see p. 35).
5. What had some of the Jews accused Paul of being (see p. 35)?
6. Although the _____ law was set aside, the _____ law has not changed (see p. 36).
7. What happens when Christians fall into legalism or libertinism (see p. 36)?
8. What is the meaning of *flesh* in the New Testament? Explain the relationship of Christian liberty to the flesh (see pp. 37-38).
9. Who are common proponents of indulging the flesh, according to Peter and Jude (see p. 38)?
10. What is the greatest liberty in the world? Who is the best example of that (see p. 39)?
11. What should be our motivation for serving God (see p. 39)?
12. As liberated Christians, how should we respond to fellow believers, according to Galatians 5:13 (see p. 40)?
13. Compare the characteristics of weak and strong Christians (see p. 40).
14. What could have made the weaker Christians in Rome stumble over eating food (see p. 41)?
15. Why should a stronger Christian not make an issue out of neutral things (see p. 42)?
16. What does it mean to cause someone to stumble (see p. 43)?
17. Rather than food, what are the important issues in the kingdom of God, according to Romans 14:17 (see p. 43)?
18. Whom should the strong Christian aim to please? Why (see p. 44)?
19. What can happen with an inconsiderate misuse of Christian liberty (see p. 44)?

20. How does Christian liberty fulfill God's moral law (see p. 45)?
21. How is the expression of Christian freedom made possible (see pp. 45-46)?

Pondering the Principles

1. Consider ways people are often enslaved to their work, their lovers, their hobbies, their bodies, or their goals to gain meaning in this life and acceptance by others. There are also those who are enslaved to a religious system. Jesus said that "everyone who commits sin is the slave of sin" (John 8:34, NASB). Praise God that He has given us the truth and that He sent His Son to make us free (vv. 32, 36). Memorize John 8:36: "If . . . the Son shall make you free, you shall be free indeed" (NASB).

2. Meditate on the sixth chapter of Romans. As Christians we have been freed from the merciless bondage of sin and given over to a new and gracious Master. Therefore, we should strive to please Him by living righteous lives. Consider the example of Christ. Paul said, "Even Christ pleased not himself" (Rom. 15:3). Christ's entire life was directed toward pleasing the Father in fulfilling His will (cf. Luke 2:49; John 4:32; 5:30; Mark 14:36). Are you committed to fulfilling the Lord's will? Prayerfully dedicate yourself to pleasing the One who has enlisted you as a "soldier of Christ Jesus" (2 Tim. 2:3-4).

4
Walking by the Spirit—Part 1

Outline

Introduction
A. The Power of the Holy Spirit
 1. Acknowledged
 2. Avoided
B. The Purpose of Paul

Lesson
I. The Command
 A. The Meaning of the Walk
 B. The Misunderstanding About the Walk
II. The Conflict
 A. Stated
  1. Defining the flesh
   a) The source of human weakness
   b) The source of Christian struggle
  2. Dealing with the flesh
   a) The source of victory acknowledged
    (1) Romans 8:3
    (2) Romans 8:26
   b) The source of victory applied
    (1) Putting on Christ
    (2) Yielding to God
    (3) Starving the flesh
     (a) Romans 8:12-13
     (b) Colossians 3:5
    (4) Being involved
     (a) Hebrews 12:1
     (b) 1 Corinthians 9:27
     (c) 2 Timothy 2:3-6
 B. Solved
  1. The role of the law
   a) Stated

    b) Supported
2. The release from the law
    a) Stated
    b) Supported
        (1) Romans 8:14
        (2) John 16:13

Introduction

Galatians 5:16-18 says, "This I say then, Walk in the Spirit, and ye shall not fulfill the lust of the flesh. For the flesh lusteth against the Spirit, and the Spirit against the flesh; and these are contrary the one to the other, so that ye cannot do the things that ye would. But if ye be led by the Spirit, ye are not under the law."

A. The Power of the Holy Spirit

    1. Acknowledged

    Anyone who knows anything about the basics of the Christian life knows that the key to living the Christian life is the Holy Spirit. At the moment of salvation the Holy Spirit takes up residence in the life of a believer and becomes the source of power for his life. The theme of the rest of Galatians 5 is the Spirit-controlled life and what it produces—the fruit of the Spirit: "love, joy, peace, long-suffering, gentleness, goodness, faith, meekness, [and] self control" (vv. 22-23). The Holy Spirit provides the power for a fruitful Christian life lived to the glory of God.

    2. Avoided

    The more legalism you apply to your Christian life, the more you hinder the work of the Holy Spirit, because you are eliminating the necessity of His ministry and creating spiritual hypocrisy. You must allow the Spirit of God to produce works of holiness as you walk in His power. There are some people who equate holiness with how many times you go to church or how often you pray or read the Bible. I knew a fellow student like that in a Christian college I attended. This college had an optional prayer meeting. I took advantage of the fact that my attendance wasn't required, exercising one of the few prerogatives the school offered. That guy trapped me in a hall one day and said, "You're not spiritual because you don't go to the optional prayer meeting!" His view of spirituality was where you went not what you were.

On another occasion I had an opportunity to teach a Sunday school class when the teacher was sick. Afterwards, a fellow came up to me and said, "That was a marvelous lesson. I didn't know you were spiritual." His measure of spirituality was whether a person was ministering to others. Unfortunately, some people think that spirituality is only where you go or what you do, rather than what's going on inside. That's legalism—attempting to equate holiness with performance.

B. The Purpose of Paul

Paul was arguing against legalism. He was saying that freedom in Christ involves allowing the Spirit of God to produce holiness and not futilely trying to attain it ourselves. He was saying that we're not under law as Christians. The legalistic Jews were shocked because they believed that without the law, sin would run rampant. The only restrainer for sin they could conceive was the law, being unaware of the Holy Spirit's internal restraint. They thought freedom from the law would burst the dam and the waters of sin would drown everyone. So Paul very carefully shows in chapters 5-6 that Christian liberty does not mean that sin runs wild. Our freedom does not mean we indulge in the flesh, injure others, or ignore the law (vv. 13-15). Rather, it fulfills the law by allowing us to serve others in love through the power of the Spirit.

How can the Christian—free from law—keep from drowning his life in sin? Galatians 5:16 gives the answer: "This I say then, Walk in [by] the Spirit, and ye shall not fulfill the lust of the flesh." Living in the power of the Spirit is basic to the Christian life. That is the theme in verses 16-25. In verses 18 and 25 he repeats that idea: "If ye be led by the Spirit, ye are not under the law. . . . If we live in the Spirit, let us also walk in the Spirit."

The Key to Holiness

Walking by the Spirit is basic to holiness. We can have holiness in our lives without legalism as we walk by the energy of the Holy Spirit, yielding to Him. That is essentially the same concept as being "strengthened with might by [the] Spirit in the inner man" (Eph. 3:16) or being "filled with the Spirit" (Eph. 5:18). The Christian does not set up a list of dos and don'ts to live a holy life. If he concentrates only on external things, he is much like the Pharisees, of whom Jesus

51

said, "You might be careful that you don't do this or that, but your thoughts are foul. You might not murder, but you hate. You might not commit adultery, but you lust after women. The evil intent of your hearts makes you guilty of murder and adultery." I've seen situations where Christians did not do specific things, but their thoughts were so corrupt that God must have been as grieved as if they had actually done them. They knew nothing of walking by the Spirit; they were experts on being circumscribed to an external ethic. They were unaware that faithfully walking by the energy of the Spirit produces the holiness of God.

If I had my choice of being obedient to an external list of rules or simply walking by the energy of an internal power, I would choose the latter. I am glad I live under the New Covenant, where practical holiness is the product of living by the energy of the indwelling Spirit. He empowers me to do the things that I couldn't force myself to do, no matter what the outside rules might be. Walking by the Spirit comes in four parts in our text: the command, the conflict, the contrast, and the conquest.

Lesson

I. THE COMMAND (v. 16)

"This I say then, Walk [by] the Spirit, and ye shall not fulfill the lust of the flesh."

How do we prevent misusing our liberty in Christ? Paul gave us a present-tense command: Continue to walk by the Spirit. The Christian walk is a daily routine. It isn't something you come to at one point in your life and say, "From now on I commit myself to walking in the Spirit." No, it's not a once-for-all event. You must be walking continuously by the Spirit so that you do not fulfill the lusts of the flesh. Even a new Christian has the wherewithal to completely fulfill God's requirements for holiness. You say, "But he doesn't know anything." He only needs to know one thing: Keep on walking by the Spirit and the Spirit will produce in him the things that God desires. It's very easy for us to excuse a new Christian for being guided by his flesh. But he has the same resource available to him that all Christians do. Sin is not usually a question of having the right information; it's a question of whether you walk in the power of the Spirit. The fulfillment of God's holiness comes in walking by the Spirit. When He comes in and controls our life, He begins to exercise our liberty in a way that never violates ourselves, others, or God. The Holy Spirit becomes our restrainer.

The Spirit is mentioned seven times in Galatians 5 by the apostle Paul. He was emphasizing that the Spirit subdues the flesh by granting the believer power over it. We will check our lusts, stimulate love, and fulfill the law not by circumscribing ourselves to an external code, but by walking by the Spirit. Unfortunately, many Christians who have fallen prey to legalistic teaching have wound up trying to live by a code that someone else set for them; therefore they never do know the meaning of victory in their lives.

A. The Meaning of the Walk

The word *walk* implies progress. It pictures a day-by-day, step-by-step existence in which a Christian yields each moment of his life to the control of the Holy Spirit. That's the key to holiness. Since every Christian possesses the Holy Spirit (Rom. 8:9), we need to submit to Him, allowing Him to control our lives. Although that sounds easy to do, it's really not. I remember a chorus I used to sing when I was a young boy that gave me the impression that the Christian life was easy. It was called "Let Go and Let God Have His Wonderful Way." It wrongly implied that all a Christian needs to do is rest in the Holy Spirit and let Him do all the work. That thinking was the emphasis of the quietistic movement.

B. The Misunderstanding About the Walk

The Quietists were late seventeenth-century mystics who believed that a one-time surrender to God would initiate a passive union with God. The Quakers were influenced by the Quietists. Even the evangelical Bible conferences at Keswick, England, were quietistic in emphasis. Hannah Whitall Smith's *The Christian's Secret to a Happy Life* (Old Tappan, N. J.: Revell, 1952) and the sermons of Charles Finney both promote the idea that a Christian needs to do little but rely on the Spirit. Quietists believe that walking in the Spirit does not require any effort on our part, and when there is effort, we hinder the holiness that God wants to accomplish. The concept of surrender in quietism is vital to living a virtuous holy life. Some, though not all, believe that when one completely surrenders, he receives a second work of grace so that the sin nature becomes eradicated and the Christian supposedly never sins again.

Although we are indebted to many of the Quietists, their teaching of a passive surrender to the Spirit is beyond Scripture. It raises the irreconcilable problem of who is at fault when you sin. You can say, "It can't be my fault because I was surrendered. And it can't be the Holy Spirit's fault because He wouldn't do something like that. Therefore, I must have taken back my surrender." That would be a sin too. Whose fault was that? Walking in the Spirit is not as simple as it sounds, although the command itself is very simple. If holy living were entirely the responsibility of God, we probably wouldn't need the command. Its presence implies that our own effort is involved in the process. What makes the command so challenging is the presence of conflict.

II. THE CONFLICT (vv. 17-18)

A. Stated (v. 17)

"For the flesh lusteth against the Spirit, and the Spirit against the flesh; and these are contrary the one to the other, so that ye cannot do the things that ye would."

Paul first said to walk by the Spirit and then said it's going to be tough because there's going to be a fight. Our walk is not simple in practice; there is a struggle involved. Even though a Christian is a new creation in Christ (2 Cor. 5:17) and has been "crucified with Christ" (Gal. 2:20), he still has the capacity to sin. That's the first thing a new Christian usually finds out. Because he still has a physical body, he still bears the sin nature. That is why Christians wait for the redemption (glorification) of the body. When we are glorified, sin won't be a problem any longer. We Christians can recognize God's will, but we still can have problems implementing it. We know God wants us to be holy and to walk by the Spirit, but achieving those ideals is a constant struggle because the flesh restricts their accomplishment. If a person is not a believer, he will not have that conflict. He will go on sinning and loving it without the presence of Holy Spirit in his life. But for the believer, there is a battle going on.

1. Defining the flesh

The word translated "flesh" (Gk., *sarx*) in this context does not refer to the body (although it's sometimes used that way; cf., Luke 24:39). It is used in the New Testament in a number of different ways.

a) The source of human weakness

54

Flesh is used in a theological sense to refer to the part of man that is easily attacked by temptation and susceptible to sin.

(1) Romans 4:1—"What shall we say, then, that Abraham, our father, as pertaining to the flesh, hath found?" The use of *flesh* there refers to Abraham's humanness, which was susceptible to sin. Paul was asking, "Did Abraham make himself righteous? No. What did his flesh produce? It didn't produce a thing." The flesh is that part of man that cannot produce anything but sin. The previous verse refers to all of Abraham's efforts apart from God.

(2) Galatians 3:3—"Are ye so foolish? Having begun in the Spirit, are ye now made perfect by the flesh?" Here again *flesh* refers to the futile effort of trying to accomplish holiness on your own.

(3) Galatians 6:12—The Judaizers wanted to make a "show in the flesh." Again the flesh is used to speak of the lower nature of man, which is incapable of righteousness apart from God.

(4) Romans 6:19—Paul speaks of "the infirmity of [the] flesh."

(5) Romans 7:18—Paul summed things up this way: "I know that in me (that is, in my flesh) dwelleth no good thing." The flesh is the part of man that functions apart from God, attempting to attain righteousness on its own.

(6) Romans 7:5—Paul speaks of "when we were in the flesh," referring to a hypothetical time before the point of salvation.

b) The source of Christian struggle

The Christian also struggles with the flesh. Even though we are new creations in Christ, we still have operating within us the propensity to function apart from God to accomplish our own ends. Romans 7 gives us good insight into the struggle that the flesh can put up against the Holy Spirit in the life of a Christian. Paul acknowledged the problem he has with the flesh. Just because a person is saved doesn't mean he is rid of that problem. That doesn't happen until he goes to heaven and gets rid of his earthly flesh, which is the beachhead of sin. In Romans 7:14 Paul says, "I am carnal [Gk., *sarx*, "fleshly"], sold under sin." Sure, I am a believer, but I've got within me a beachhead on which the forces of Satan always land; temptation always gets me there. The flesh creates a terrible tension in a Christian as it wars against the Holy Spirit—and sometimes gains victory. In verses 15-16 Paul says, "That which I do I understand not; for what I would, that do I not; but what I hate, that do I. If, then, I do that which I would not, I consent unto the law that it is good." In other words, "There's nothing wrong with God's law. It's not His fault that I've got a problem." Then Paul said, "It is no more I that do it, but sin that dwelleth in me" (v. 17). There is a sin principle operating in the flesh. Paul continued, "I know that in me (that is, in my flesh) dwelleth no good thing; for to will is present with me, but how to perform that which is good I find not. For the good that I would, I do not; but the evil which I would not, that I do" (vv. 18-19). Paul was saying, "I have the desire; I just can't put it into practice." If that isn't the testimony of the Christian life at times, I don't know what is! Some people identify Romans 7 as Paul's struggle before he became a Christian. But no unsaved man in the world has the problem of struggling against the law of God in his heart. Verses 21-25 say, "I find then a law, that, when I would do good, evil is present with me. For I delight in the law of God after the inward man; but I see another law in my members, warring against the law of my mind, and bringing me into captivity to the law of sin which is in my members. Oh, wretched man that I am! Who shall deliver me from the body of this death? I thank God through Jesus Christ, our Lord." Paul stated that the answer to this dilemma is in Christ, and he expounds on that in chapter 8. Paul sums up the struggle in verse 25: "So, then, with the mind I myself serve the law of God; but with the flesh, the law of sin." He defines the flesh as that part of a Christian that serves sin.

The flesh refers to the spiritual part of me that offers ineffective natural effort, independent of God, and is the place where sin lands and does its work. Galatians 5:17 tells us that the flesh lusts against the

Spirit. Although we often think of lust as connected with sin, the verb actually means "to desire strongly." It conveys the idea of contesting or struggling to accomplish something. So the flesh is struggling against the Spirit to dominate the believer.

2. Dealing with the flesh

   a) The source of victory acknowledged

   It is not nearly as important to be concerned with what the devil is doing as to be concerned with your own flesh. Rather than worrying about the strategy of Satan, you ought to positively entertain yourself with the concept of putting on Jesus Christ and walking by the Spirit. Then everything will take care of itself. Fortunately, the Spirit wants to operate in our lives. Every time the flesh starts doing its thing, the Spirit begins to combat the flesh. It's good to know that our flesh is being countered by the Spirit. Therefore, Christians should recognize that victory is available.

   (1) Romans 8:3—Paul said God has done for us "what the law could not do, in that it was weak through the flesh." The flesh is weak, but the Spirit of God is powerful. It's good to know that you have residing in you the absolute power of God fighting against the weakness of the flesh. So if you sin, it's because you gave up. You can't say, "The fight was on, and the flesh won. I was rooting for the Spirit all the way. I don't know what happened." No, both sides don't have the same degree of strength. The Spirit is all powerful.

   (2) Romans 8:26—Paul told us that "the Spirit also helps our weakness" (NASB). If we ally ourselves with the Spirit, there will always be a victory.

   b) The source of victory applied

   (1) Putting on Christ

   The Christian has to deal with the flesh, which carries on work that is counterproductive to spiritual growth. Therefore, Paul provided a positive instruction for productive Christian living: "Walk [by] the Spirit, and ye shall not fulfill the lust of the flesh." You may ask how one walks by the Spirit. Romans 13:13-14 is a parallel passage that deals with living by legalism as opposed to living by the Spirit and fulfilling the whole law by love. It offers good insight into the meaning of the Christian walk: "Let us walk honestly, as in the day [where our life can be exposed]; not in reveling and drunkenness, not in immorality and wantonness [shamelessness], not in strife and envying. But put ye on the Lord Jesus Christ, and make not provision for the flesh, to fulfill its lusts." The fact that putting on the Lord Jesus Christ and walking in the Spirit both result in not fulfilling the lusts of the flesh implies that they are essentially the same thing. The Spirit-filled life of walking by the Spirit is the equivalent to living a Christlike life. Walking by the Spirit involves saturating my life with the person of Christ. He should dominate my thought patterns as I live in the consciousness of His presence. Since the Spirit's work is to point to Christ, walking by the Spirit means that my life is patterned after the Lord Jesus Christ. The more I study the gospels and come to know Jesus Christ, the more fulfilling the Christian life becomes to me. Paul had the same goal. He said, "That I may know him" (Phil. 3:10).

I'm not talking about some kind of passive knowledge. You can't be a Quietist, saying, "I'm just going to wait until the spiritual battle is all over." At some point you've got to get in the battle, as Scripture indicates.

(2) Yielding to God

Romans 6:12 says, "Let not sin, therefore, reign in your mortal body." That is not a command to the Holy Spirit; it's a command to us. God is telling Christians not to let sin control their lives. The presence of the command indicates that we can do something about it. Paul continued by saying that we're not to "obey it in its lusts. Neither yield ye your members as instruments of unrighteousness unto sin, but yield yourselves unto God, as those that are alive from the dead, and your members as instruments of righteousness unto God" (vv. 12-13). We must determine

58

to yield ourselves to the Holy Spirit rather than to our fleshly desires. However, though we rest in the Spirit's power, we must also get into the action.

(3) Starving the flesh

    (a) Romans 8:12-13—"Therefore, brethren, we are debtors, not to the flesh, to live after the flesh" (v. 12). Do you owe the flesh anything? Did the flesh ever do anything for you? No one ever gives a testimony on how the flesh has blessed his life. There is no reason to pay any kind of attention to the flesh. We have been liberated at the cross from being controlled by our fleshly desires. Verse 13 says, "If ye live after the flesh, ye shall die; but if ye, through the Spirit, do mortify the deeds of the body, ye shall live." Paul says, "Get in there and kill the flesh!" The best way to do that is to starve it to death. If you refuse to feed it anything, it shrivels up. If you feed the flesh, you put yourself in a position to be tempted. But don't give it anything that appeals to it. Walking by the Spirit is not a state of passive surrender; we must be actively involved in controlling our flesh.

    (b) Colossians 3:5—"Put to death, therefore, whatever belongs to your earthly nature: sexual immorality, impurity, lust, evil desires and greed, which is idolatry" (NIV*). We must be actively engaged in rendering inoperative every ungodly desire.

(4) Being involved

The Christian life is not a spectator sport. Many verses in the New Testament make that clear.

    (a) Hebrews 12:1—"Wherefore, seeing we also are compassed about with so great a cloud of witnesses . . . let us run with patience the race that is set before us."

*New International Version.

59

(b) 1 Corinthians 9:27—The apostle Paul pictured himself in a boxing match in the Christian life: "I beat my body and make it my slave" (NIV). He wasn't passive in his Christian walk. The Christian must be actively involved.

(c) 2 Timothy 2:3-6—"Thou, therefore, endure hardness, as a good soldier of Jesus Christ. No man that warreth entangleth himself with the affairs of this life, that he may please him who hath chosen him to be a soldier. And if a man also strive for masteries [as an athlete], yet is he not crowned, except he strive lawfully. The farmer that laboreth must be first partaker of the fruits." The Christian is to be like a dedicated soldier, a runner who wants to win, and a hard-working farmer. That kind of commitment demands involvement. The Christian life is not something I watch; it is something I am totally absorbed in.

The Paradox of Spiritual Life

An apparent contradiction of Christian living is that while my life is not mine but Christ's, at the same time I am living it (Gal. 2:20). Then who lives your Christian life: you or the Holy Spirit? It is all by the Spirit's power, but it demands all our yieldedness and commitment. I am responsible to put to death my fleshly desires. I don't know how the combination works, but I do know that when I sin, I never blame the Holy Spirit. Anyone who does has something grossly wrong with his theology, because God has no part in sin. The opposite extreme of quietism is pietism, the religion of self effort. There must be a balance found in walking by the Spirit. Walking in the Spirit involves yielding to the Holy Spirit and killing sin.

B. Solved (v. 18)

"But if ye be led by the Spirit, ye are not under the law."

1. The role of the law

a) Stated

Why did Paul say we are not under the law? Because under the law we couldn't conquer the flesh. But if we walk by the Spirit (v. 16) we will have no problem

60

with the flesh, and if we're led by the Spirit we will have no problem with the law. To be under the law is to be unable to stop the lusts of the flesh. The law cannot stop sin; it stirs it up and reveals it. Paul makes that clear in Romans 7:8-10: "But sin, taking occasion by the commandment, wrought in me all manner of coveting. . . . For I was alive apart from the law once; but when the commandment came, sin revived, and I died. And the commandment, which was ordained to life, I found to be unto death." In other words, "God showed me His beautiful law, and it killed me because I couldn't keep it."

b) Supported

If you are being led by the Spirit, you are no longer under the terrible curse of the law because the Spirit fulfills the law and conquers the flesh. Trying to obey the law on your own doesn't do anything but make a mess. In the classic *Pilgrim's Progress*, we find the Interpreter's House, where there is a large room full of dust. When a man in the room starts sweeping the dust with a broom, Christian, the main character of the allegory, begins coughing. The Interpreter explains, "This parlour is the heart of a man that was never sanctified . . . the dust is his original sin. . . . He that began to sweep at first, is the Law; but she that brought water, and did sprinkle it, is the Gospel" (John Bunyan [Springdale, Pa.: Whitaker House, 1981], p. 31).

First Corinthians 15:56 says, "The strength of sin is the law." The law reveals sin to be what it is. If there is no law, sin cannot be identified. So when the law comes, you automatically sin. There is no capacity to obey the law. An illustration of the way the law provokes sin is given by Pete Gillquist in his book *Love Is Now* (Grand Rapids: Zondervan, 1970, p. 131). Suppose there are two houses built across town from each other, each having a big plate glass window. If one owner puts a sign on his lawn that reads, "Do not break the window," whose window do you think will get broken first? The law has a certain provocative quality.

2. The release from the law

   a) Stated

However, if you are led by the Spirit, you are no longer left under the law to be provoked to sin. Being led by the Spirit means basically the same thing as walking by the Spirit, but it does emphasize something else: that the Spirit is actively leading.

b) Supported

(1) Romans 8:14—"As many as are led by the Spirit of God, they are the sons of God." Every Christian is being led by the Spirit. You don't need to pray, "Holy Spirit, lead me." He is doing that. Rather, you ought to ask Him to teach you how to follow. If you have the Holy Spirit living in you, you are not under the penalty of law. God only gives His Spirit to people who have accepted Him by grace. Everyone else is under the law. Those who would like to be out from under the law and the wrath of God need to accept Jesus Christ, who will then give them His Spirit. That you are led by the Spirit means you are no longer under the system of law. Everyone in the world is under one of the two systems: They are either under the Spirit or under the law.

(2) John 16:13—The Holy Spirit guides us into truth. He leads every Christian. We are not under the law; we are under the Spirit's leading—not external, but internal direction.

If the Holy Spirit is leading us, our responsibility is to walk where He leads (Gal. 5:16). The blind man of Jericho was led to Jesus in Luke 18. If you just pointed the way to a blind man, that wouldn't do him much good. You would have to take him by the hand and lead him. When the Holy Spirit comes into the life of a believer He will lead that new Christian. As a Christian follows the Spirit, he will not fulfill the lusts of the flesh.

Where does the Holy Spirit lead me?

There are eight places to which the Holy Spirit leads you:

1. To freedom (Gal. 5:1)
2. To holiness (2 Thess. 2:13)
3. To the Word of Truth (John 16:14)
4. To fruitfulness (Gal. 5:22-23)
5. To prayer (Eph. 2:18)

If you are walking by the Spirit, you don't need a set of rules because the Spirit is doing the leading. The Galatians had stopped following the Spirit and started following the flesh. Don't do that. Romans 8:3-4 says, "What the law could not do, in that it was weak through the flesh, God sending his own Son, in the likeness of sinful flesh and for sin, condemned sin in the flesh, that the righteousness of the law might be fulfilled in us, who walk not after the flesh, but after the Spirit." God wants to accomplish the law in our lives as we walk in the Spirit.

Focusing on the Facts

1. When does the Holy Spirit take up residence in the life of a believer (see p. 50)?
2. What happens when a Christian applies legalism to his life? Why (see p. 50)?
3. What did legalistic Jews think would happen if the law was set aside (see p. 51)?
4. What does the present-tense command Paul gives us in Galatians 5:16 tell us about the nature of walking in the Spirit (see p. 52)?
5. What idea does the word *walk* imply? What is the key to holiness in the Christian walk (see p. 53)?
6. How have some people misunderstood the nature of the Christian walk? What theological problems result from that misunderstanding (see pp. 53-54)?
7. Is walking by the Spirit a simple practice? Explain (see p. 54).
8. When will Christians no longer have a problem with sin (see p. 54)?
9. Why is an unbeliever not aware of the conflict between the flesh and the Spirit (see p. 54)?
10. Even though Christians are new creations in Christ, what do they still have operating within them (see p. 55)?
11. What part of a person does the *flesh* refer to (see pp. 55-56)?
12. Is it more important to be concerned with your flesh or with what the devil is doing? Explain (see p. 57).
13. Why must the Christian deal with the flesh (see p. 57)?
14. What, in addition to walking by the Spirit, results in not fulfilling the lusts of the flesh (Rom. 13:14; see p. 58)?

15. How can a Christian "mortify the deeds of the body" (Rom. 8:13; see p. 59)?
16. Cite examples from Scripture that show that the Christian life is not a spectator sport (see pp. 59-60).
17. Identify the paradox of spiritual life (see p. 60).
18. Rather than stopping sin, what does the law do to it (Rom. 7:8-10; see p. 61)?
19. If you are being led by the Spirit, why are you no longer under "the curse of the law" (Gal. 3:13; see p. 61)?
20. When the Holy Spirit leads us, what is our responsibility as Christians (see p. 62)?
21. Where does the Spirit lead believers (see pp. 62-63)?

Pondering the Principles

1. Are you really walking by the Spirit? The word *walk* implies step-by-step progress. Are you accepting your responsibility to follow His leading one step at a time, or are you waiting for the Spirit to hurl you into a quantum leap? Many people want others to solve their problems for them because of their lack of discipline and determination. That philosophy is not uncommon in Christian circles. Don't expect the Spirit to miraculously make you holy. Holiness is a joint effort: The Spirit leads, but you must follow. Scripture teaches that we are involved in the growth process. We must discipline ourselves to work toward greater holiness on a daily basis. Make prayer and meditation on Scripture a regular part of your Christian walk as you let the Spirit lead you to the throne of grace and through the Word of God. As you are led, remember to follow.

2. Read Colossians 3:5. What earthly desires do you need to put to death? Have you been feeding those desires with pornography, lustful fantasies, or materialistic attitudes? Paul says, "Clothe yourselves with the Lord Jesus Christ, and do not think about how to gratify the desires of the sinful nature" (Rom. 13:14, NIV). With temptation so readily available in our materialistic and self-indulgent society, be prepared to run from things that will hinder your spiritual development, defraud others, and grieve the God who calls you to be holy (1 Thess. 4:1-8).

5

Walking by the Spirit—Part 2

Outline

Introduction
A. The Christian Walk Defined
B. The Christian Walk Delineated

Review
I. The Command
  A. The Meaning of the Walk
    1. The means compared
      a) The filling of the Spirit
      b) The indwelling of the Word
    2. The mediators compared
      a) The replacement for Christ
      b) The walk in Christ
  B. The Misunderstanding About the Walk
II. The Conflict
  A. Stated
  B. Solved
    1. The role of the law
    2. The release from the law
      a) Stated
      b) Supported
      c) Specified
        (1) Its presence
        (2) Its power
        (3) Its penalty

Lesson
III. The Contrast
  A. The Works of the Flesh
    1. The categories
      a) Sex
        (1) Fornication

      (2) Uncleanness
      (3) Lasciviousness
  b) Religion
      (1) Idolatry
      (2) Sorcery
  c) Relationships
  d) Alcohol
2. The consequence

Introduction

A. **The Christian Walk Defined**

Galatians 5:16-25 is the primary passage in Scripture on walking by the Spirit, a basic concept of the Christian life. The word *walk* is often used in the New Testament to refer to the practical daily life of a believer. If you wanted to use a contemporary synonym for *walk*, you could use the word *life-style*.

B. **The Christian Walk Delineated**

1. **Humility**

Our life-style is to be characterized by humility. Ephesians 4:2-3 says, "With all lowliness and meekness, with long-suffering, forbearing one another in love, endeavoring to keep the unity of the Spirit in the bond of peace." There's only one thing that produces unity and that's love—and love is the product of humility.

2. **Purity**

The New Testament also exhorts the believer to have a pure life-style. Romans 13:13 says, "Let us behave decently, as in the daytime, not in orgies and drunkenness, not in sexual immorality and debauchery, not in dissension and jealousy" (NIV).

3. **Contentment**

First Corinthians 7:17 says, "As God hath distributed to every man, as the Lord hath called every one, so let him walk." The context of the passage deals with marital status. If a person is saved but is married to an unsaved spouse, that is not grounds to dissolve the marriage. Rather, that person is to be content to walk in the way that God has called him. Don't end a marriage with a spiritual excuse; be content. God knows your situation and has allowed it to work out the way it has. Marriage is just one way in which we are to walk in contentment.

4. Faith

Second Corinthians 5:7 says, "We walk by faith, not by sight." The believer is not to evaluate things that are happening by what he actually sees but in terms of his faith in God. He should interpret everything from a heavenly perspective. He sees God at work in spite of the circumstances.

5. Good works

Colossians 1:10 says, "Walk worthy of the Lord unto all pleasing, being fruitful in every good work." Ephesians 2:10 says, "We are his workmanship, created in Christ Jesus unto good works, which God hath before ordained that we should walk in them."

6. Transformation

Ephesians 4:17-23 tells us that Christians are to walk differently from unbelievers. Verse 17 says, "This I say, therefore, and testify in the Lord, that you henceforth walk not as other Gentiles walk, in the vanity of their mind." The Christian is not to live like those in the world do. His transformed life should be different. Verses 18-23 contrast the old walk of an unbeliever with the new walk of a Christian.

   a) Christ-centeredness

   The old walk of "the vanity of [the] mind" was self-centered. But Christians "have not so learned Christ" (v. 20). The new walk is a Christ-centered walk.

   b) Enlightenment

   The old walk was characterized by ignorance. Verse 18 describes unbelievers as "having [their] understanding darkened, being alienated from the life of God through the ignorance that is in them, because of the blindness of their heart." However, the new walk is characterized by knowledge. Verse 21 says, "If so be that ye have heard him, and have been taught by him, as the truth is in Jesus." Christians have been taught the truth of Christ through His Spirit.

c) Sensitivity to sin

The conscience of an unbeliever is insensitive to sin. Verse 19 says that "being past feeling, [unbelievers] have given themselves over unto lasciviousness." In contrast to unbelievers who shamelessly pursue uncleanness, the new walk of believers is characterized by a sensitivity to sin. Verse 22 says, "Put off concerning the former manner of life the old man, which is corrupt according to the deceitful lusts."

d) A renewed mind

Our old walk was directed by a reprobate mind that was completely given over "to work all uncleanness with greediness" (v. 19). It knew no limits. However, the believer is "renewed in the spirit of [his] mind" (v. 23). The old walk and the new walk are diametrically opposed.

7. Separation

We are to separate ourselves not only from the world, but also from sinning Christians. In 2 Thessalonians 3, Paul says, "We command you, brethren, in the name of our Lord Jesus Christ, that ye withdraw yourselves from every brother that walketh disorderly and not after the tradition which he received of us. For ye yourselves know how ye ought to follow us; for we behaved not ourselves disorderly among you. . . . For we hear that there are some who walk among you disorderly, working not at all but are busybodies" (vv. 6-7, 11). We are to separate ourselves from Christians living in sin.

8. Love

Ephesians 5:2 says, "Walk in love, as Christ also hath loved us, and hath given himself for us an offering and a sacrifice to God." We are to express the kind of love that sacrifices itself for the benefit of others. The world thinks of love in a physical, self-serving sense, but that is nothing more than "fornication, and all uncleanness" (v. 3). We are to love as Christ loved—sacrificially.

9. Light

Ephesians 5:8 says, "Ye were once darkness, but now are ye light in the Lord; walk as children of light."

10. Wisdom

Ephesians 5:15-16 says, "See, then, that ye walk circum-

spectly [carefully], not as fools but as wise, redeeming the
time, because the days are evil" (cf., Col. 4:5).

11. Truth

Third John 3-4 says, "I rejoiced greatly, when the brethren came and testified of the truth that is in thee, even as
thou walkest in the truth. I have no greater joy than to
hear that my children walk in truth." If you are a teacher
or a discipler of others, you can understand the joy in
finding your students or disciples living by the truths you
have taught them. The greatest disappointment is to find
out that they are not.

Review

Everything becomes ultimately possible in the Christian walk because
the Spirit of God is in us as we take each step. All we need to do is
walk in His power and He will conform us to Christ. You can grunt
and groan in your own power as you try legalistically to be like Christ.
But Paul has been telling us that you cannot attain the righteousness
that God demands through legalism. The law can't save or sanctify
you. It is the Spirit of God who saves you, secures you, and sanctifies
you. You were saved by grace and continue to stand by grace (cf.,
Rom. 5:1-2). You don't need to live by external works of the law to be
accepted by God, which is what the Judaizers tried to teach. You
don't need outward rituals when you have God dwelling within you
(cf., 1 Cor. 6:19).

The immediate context in Galatians is Paul's reaction to the Judaizers.
He has told the Galatians that the Christian doesn't need to live under
a legal system. The Judaizers believed that the penalty of the law
restrained people from sinning. With Paul's message of Christian
liberty, they were afraid that without the law, there would be no
restraint for sin. But Paul told the Galatians that the restraint has
become internal: the Holy Spirit has become our conscience and
enables us to live godly lives.

I. THE COMMAND (v. 16)

A. The Meaning of the Walk (see p. 53)

Walking by the Spirit implies daily progress and effort on our
part as well as power and direction on God's part. Since this
concept is somewhat abstract, the Holy Spirit accommodates
our thinking by repeatedly making a comparison for us in the
New Testament.

1. The means compared

    a) The filling of the Spirit

    Ephesians 5:18 says, "Be not drunk with wine, in
    which is excess, but be filled with the Spirit." The
    Greek text implies that the filling of the Spirit is a
    continuous exercise. In a more literal sense the verse
    would read, "Be being kept filled with the Spirit."
    The filling of Spirit is the same thing as walking by
    the Spirit, which involves yielding control of your life
    to the indwelling Spirit of God. The command "be
    filled" conveys the idea of wind filling a ship's sail so
    that it carries the ship along. Paul might as well have
    said, "Open the sail of your will in submission and be
    carried along by the Spirit."

    Notice the results of being Spirit-filled: you'll be
    "speaking to yourselves in psalms and hymns and
    spiritual songs, singing and making melody in your
    heart to the Lord" (v. 19). A Spirit-filled person
    expresses his joy by singing—even if he can't carry a
    tune. He also gives thanks (v. 20) and submits to
    others (v. 21). Spirit-filled wives submit to their
    husbands (v. 22), Spirit-filled husbands love their
    wives (v. 25), Spirit-filled children obey their parents
    (6:1), Spirit-filled parents do not provoke their chil-
    dren to anger (6:4), Spirit-filled servants are obedient
    to their masters (6:5), and Spirit-filled masters are fair
    to their servants (6:9).

    b) The indwelling of the Word

    The results of the filling of the Spirit found in
    Colossians 3:16—4:1 are almost identical to those
    listed above. Colossians 3:16 says, "In all wisdom
    teaching and admonishing one another, in psalms
    and hymns and spiritual songs singing with grace in
    your hearts to the Lord. And whatever ye do in word
    or deed, do all in the name of the Lord Jesus, giving
    thanks to God." The following verses speak of the
    submission of wives (v. 18), husbands (v. 19), chil-
    dren (v. 20), fathers (v. 21), servants (v. 22), and
    masters or employers (4:1). These same results, how-
    ever, are said to be the product of letting "the word of
    Christ dwell in you richly" (3:16). Therefore, what-
    ever it means to be filled with the Spirit is related to
    letting "the word of Christ dwell in you richly."

Being Spirit-filled means taking the Bible and studying about Christ until He saturates your being.

2. The mediators compared

   a) The replacement for Christ

   It may sound that Christ is being confused with the Holy Spirit, but in fact they are of the same essence as co-equal members of the Trinity. Jesus told His disciples that when He ascended to heaven, the Father would send "another Comforter" (John 14:16). The Greek word *allos* ("another of the same kind") was used rather than *heteros* ("another of a different kind"). Jesus promised to send the Holy Spirit, who is exactly the same essence as He is. Furthermore, the Holy Spirit is called "the Spirit of Christ" (Rom. 8:9).

   Living a Spirit-filled life or filling your mind with Scripture will cause your thought patterns to be directed by the Spirit. I used to enjoy sinning, but I don't enjoy it anymore. I can't get five seconds into a sin without thinking of fifteen convicting Bible verses. I have studied so many Bible verses that sin is no fun anymore. I feel guilty even before I actually commit the sin. Having your mind saturated by the things of Christ will allow your life to be easily borne along by the Spirit.

   b) The walk in Christ

   In Galatians 5:16 Paul exhorts us to "walk [by] the Spirit," but in Colossians 2:6 he says, "As ye have, therefore, received Christ Jesus the Lord, so walk ye in him." You may wonder whom you should walk by: the Spirit or the Lord Jesus Christ. But walking by the Spirit and walking in Christ are the same thing. Walking by the Spirit involves patterning your life after Christ. All you need to do is open your Bible and study for the rest of your life about His work and His person. Your whole life should be centered on Jesus Christ. It is the Spirit's work to point to Christ. Therefore, if you are walking by the Spirit, you are automatically focusing on Christ.

B. The Misunderstanding About the Walk (see pp. 53-54)

II. THE CONFLICT (vv. 17-18)

A. Stated (v. 17; see pp. 54-60)

Walking by the Spirit is not an easy task. Just as soon as you begin to walk by the Spirit, there's an enemy that will oppose you: the flesh. It is the weak, self-oriented nature of man. That's where temptation strikes.

B. Solved (v. 18)

1. The role of the law (see pp. 60-61)

2. The release from the law

    a) Stated (see pp. 60-61)

    Paul tells us that those who are led by the Spirit have been released from the law. Since all Christians are led by the Spirit, they are therefore not under the law.

    b) Supported (see p. 61)

    c) Specified

    There are three shades of meaning about the nature of our release from the law.

    (1) Its presence

    As a Christian, I don't need the law to externally motivate me to obey God. If I'm led by the Spirit, the law is superfluous. Romans 13 teaches that the whole law is fulfilled in my life as the Spirit produces a love in me for my neighbor.

    (2) Its power

    For an unbeliever the only thing that can prevent sin is the law. However, it is an ineffective restrainer because it cannot change a man's nature. According to Romans 7:13, it reveals sin as a failure to keep God's standard. A man under the law futilely tries to keep it in his flesh. But a Christian does not try to overcome his fleshly desires in his own power; he overcomes them in the power of the Spirit.

    (3) Its penalty

    The law has no claim on you, because Christ died to pay the penalty your sin deserves. As long as you walk in the Spirit, there's going to be ultimate victory. Even though we may occasionally lose a conflict, the law has no claim on us.

Lesson

III. THE CONTRAST (vv. 19-23)

Paul contrasted the different results of living by the Spirit and living by the flesh. One reason he made that contrast is to motivate Christians to walk by the Spirit. The works of the flesh are described in verses 19-21. The result of walking by the Spirit is found in verses 22-23. Paul strengthened his case for walking in the Spirit by showing what each produces. The Judaizers should have taken note of that. If they had carefully examined the Galatian churches, they would have seen the fruit of the Spirit and realized how pointless it was to introduce law. Once they introduced law, they would have seen the works of the flesh and recognized their error if they had been sensitive.

A. The Works of the Flesh (vv. 19-21)

The works of the flesh do not merely include the various misuses of sex. It is a much wider concept, including all the sinful desires of man's fallen nature. This particular list is not exhaustive but only suggestive.

Who's to Blame: You or Your Environment?

In Mark 7:20-23 Jesus speaks about the nature of original sin: "That which cometh out of the man, that defileth the man. For from within, out of the heart of men, proceed evil thoughts, adulteries, fornications, murders, thefts, covetousness, wickedness, deceit, lasciviousness, an evil eye, blasphemy, pride, foolishness. All these evil things come from within, and defile the man." Did you know that it is not the environment that messes up man; rather, it's man that messes up the environment? There are basically two anthropological explanations for man's condition: Either man is corrupted by a dirty environment, or man corrupts the environment because he is dirty himself. If you take the latter view, which is the biblical one, you'll discover that man's environment does not ultimately affect man's heart. Better housing, transportation, jobs, income, welfare, and hospitalization will not make a lasting or significant change on mankind itself. Whatever man's environment, he will foul it up, because his flesh produces the vile things that adversely affect his environment.

1. The categories (vv. 19-21a)

"Now the works of the flesh are manifest, which are

these: adultery, fornication, uncleanness, lasciviousness, idolatry, sorcery, hatred, strife, jealousy, wrath, factions, seditions, heresies, envyings, murders, drunkenness, revelings, and the like."

By saying that "the works of the flesh are manifest," Paul is appealing to common knowledge. He divided the fleshly pursuits in the normal life of mankind into four categories.

a) Sex

(1) Fornication

Since the word *adultery* does not appear in the most reliable Greek manuscripts, we'll skip that specific sexual sin and consider the more general word for any illicit sexual immorality. The Greek word for fornication is *porneia*, which some believe is derived from *pernēmi*, referring to intercourse with a prostitute for a fee. Fornication refers to any kind of sexual vice. It is one of the things that the flesh produces when left to itself.

(*a*) 1 Corinthians 5:1—"It is reported commonly that there is fornication among you, and such fornication as is not so much as named among the Gentiles, that one should have his father's wife." Paul condemned the incestuous relationship one Corinthian was having with his stepmother.

(*b*) 1 Corinthians 6:13, 18—"Foods for the body, and the body for foods; but God shall destroy both it and them. Now the body is not for fornication, but for the Lord; and the Lord for the body. . . . Flee fornication."

(*c*) 1 Corinthians 7:1-2—"Now concerning the things about which ye wrote unto me, it is good for a man not to touch a woman. Nevertheless, to avoid fornication, let every man have his own wife, and let every woman have her own husband."

(*d*) 1 Thessalonians 4:3—"This is the will of God, even your sanctification, that ye should abstain from fornication."

(e) Ephesians 5:3—"But fornication, and all uncleanness, or covetousness, let it not be once named among you, as becometh saints."

The Christian is to run from all forms of sexual sin, many of which have become commonplace in our society.

(2) Uncleanness

This word means "impurity." It was used in other ancient writings to refer to pus that oozed from an unclean wound. The root of the Greek word translated *uncleanness* (*akatharsia*) is *katharos* (from which we get *catharsis*, "purification"), and it means "pure." It was used to speak of the ceremonial cleanliness that entitled a person to approach his god. Conversely the negative form of that word referred to the soiled life of one who was unable to approach his god. Being a broader term than fornication, which emphasizes the deed, uncleanness also includes the attitude that led to the deed.

(3) Lasciviousness

Lasciviousness and wantonness are archaic words that refer to a complete lack of restraint, a common characterization of much of our society. The Greek word *aselgeia* conveys the idea of someone who has gone so far in lust he doesn't even care what anyone else thinks.

The flesh produces those sinful qualities. They marked Paul's day and mark our own as well. Man hasn't changed.

b) Religion

Whenever it is based on self effort, religion can be just as much a work of the flesh as sex. There are basically two systems of religion: One is based on human achievement and the other is based on divine grace. If a person isn't depending on divine grace, which is unique to Christianity, he is ultimately depending on what he himself can accomplish to merit salvation. In many cases, a religious system of works is more insidious than sexual perversions.

(1) Idolatry

Idolatry means worshiping an image or god. It encompasses any false religion.

(2) Sorcery

The Greek word for sorcery, *pharmakeia* (from which we get *pharmacy*), always refers to drugs, which were commonly associated with false religions. Although many people think drugs were invented recently they have actually been around for centuries. Drugs were used in the practice of occultic sorcery.

If you were to read a description of the Baal worship of the Canaanites, you would find many similarities with what is going on in Satan worship today. Little has changed. Drugs, sex, and black magic are still a part of religious perversion. Prophets like Isaiah and Ezekiel and ancient writers like Aristotle and Polybius speak of the relationship between witchcraft and drugs. In the end times, the religion of Satan will be associated with sorcery (Rev. 9:21). Today drugs play a big part in Satanic religious experience. When faith in magic replaces trust in God, the result is idolatry.

The flesh not only defiles man's relationship to himself through sexual sin, his relationship to God through religious sin, but it also devastates his relationship with others.

c) Relationships

(1) Hatred

Hatred is the opposite of love. It is the expression of enmity or hostility toward others.

(2) Strife

This word includes fighting or quarreling. Whereas hatred is the attitude, strife is the action.

(3) Jealousy

This is the anger produced by your desire to have what someone else has.

(4) Wrath

Wrath is the outburst of hostile feelings, the product of an uncontrolled temper. Like strife, it points to the action that is produced in compari-

76

son to hatred and jealousy, which emphasize the attitudes that motivate the actions. Where there is hatred, there is going to be strife. Where there is jealousy, there is going to be an outburst of temper. Human relationships are detroyed by the flesh.

(5) Factions

Once hatred and strife are in operation, people start lining up on different sides, creating terrible factions. We see people organizing for causes to fight against others throughout the world.

(6) Seditions

This refers to divisions.

(7) Heresies

This is false doctrine.

(8) Envyings

Some Greek manuscripts include murder as a climax in the list of fleshly works that destroy human relationships.

d) Alcohol

(1) Drunkenness

(2) Revelings

This refers to drinking parties. It is easy for a person living in the flesh to let himself be controlled by inanimate objects. Public orgies were common in Baal worship among the Canaanites. When the Romans came to Palestine, they built a temple to Bacchus, the god of wine, and wild orgies took place there. Some of those temples still stand today and are identified by the grape vines on the facade of the buildings. Drunken orgies were characteristic of pagan life and are reflected in many of the parties people have today.

2. The consequence (v. 21b)

"Of which I tell you before, as I have also told you in time past, that they who do such things shall not inherit the kingdom of God."

Some people wonder if that verse means a Christian can

lose his salvation if he has ever done any of those things. Although the King James Version says, "They who do such things shall not inherit the kingdom of God," the Greek word for *do* is *prassō*, which means "to practice." It is a verb that speaks of habitual practice rather than occasional doing. Thus, the verse refers to those who habitually practice such things as an expression of their characters. The word of God bases its evaluation of a person's character not on his infrequent actions, but on his habitual actions, for they demonstrate his true character. The people who habitually perform the works of the flesh will not inherit the kingdom because they are not God's people.

Some Christians may do some of those things infrequently, but that doesn't mean they will forfeit the full salvation of the kingdom of God. Rather they will receive divine discipline now and forfeit some of their heavenly rewards. The reason Christians do not habitually do the works of the flesh is that the Spirit of God has effected a change in their lives. Kingdom people led by the Spirit are characterized by the fruit of the Spirit. Christians will sin, but the course of their life will be different. You may say, "I know a guy who claims to be a Christian, and he sins frequently." In that case I doubt he is a Christian because in the believer the flesh is restrained, whereas in the unbeliever it is not.

If you fit in with those who practice any of the works of the flesh, you had better reevaluate whether you are really a Christian. You may say, "I've never actually committed fornication, even though I think about it all the time." Jesus said, "Whosoever looketh on a woman to lust after her hath committed adultery with her already in his heart" (Matt. 5:28). Remember that it's out of the vileness of your thoughts that evil deeds come (Mark 7:15). When you get into the right circumstances, your defiled thoughts will express themselves. You'll be no more vile by committing a sin than by letting it conquer your mind. If your life is characterized by any of the works of the flesh, you need to determine whether you know Christ. If you are a Christian, the Spirit will be restraining the sin in you. Christians are different because they walk by the Spirit.

78

Focusing on the Facts

1. How is the word *walk* used in reference to Christianity? What is a contemporary synonym for it (see p. 66)?
2. What does the unity of the Spirit produce, according to Ephesians 4:2-3 (see p. 66)?
3. If one marriage partner becomes a Christian while the other remains an unbeliever, what should the Christian do (1 Cor. 7:17; see p. 66)?
4. How should a believer interpret the circumstances of daily life (2 Cor. 5:7; see p. 67)?
5. Explain how the walk of the new man is different from that of the old man (Eph. 4:17-23; see pp. 67-68).
6. Whom does Paul instruct us to separate ourselves from in 2 Thessalonians 3:6-7 (see p. 68)?
7. Describe the kind of love we are to express as Christians (see p. 68).
8. If you are a teacher or a discipler of others, what brings you joy (see p. 69)?
9. How does a Christian become filled with the Spirit? What idea does the command "be filled" convey (Eph. 5:18; see p. 70)?
10. What can one conclude from comparing the results of being filled with the Spirit and letting the Word of Christ dwell in you (see pp. 70-71)?
11. Walking by the Spirit involves _____ your life after _____. How does a Christian do that (see p. 71)?
12. Why is the law an ineffective restrainer for sin (see p. 72)?
13. Why are Christians free from the penalty of the law (see p. 72)?
14. In a general sense, to what do the works of the flesh refer (see p. 73)?
15. To what did Jesus attribute the defilement of man in Mark 7:20-23 (see p. 73)?
16. Besides the misuse of sex, what other categories are included in the works of the flesh (see pp. 74-77)?
17. What have drugs commonly been associated with (see p. 76)?
18. What works of the flesh result in factions (see p. 77)?
19. Who will not inherit the kingdom of God, according to the proper understanding of the Greek word *prassō* in Galatians 5:21 (see pp. 77-78)?
20. On what does the Word of God base the evaluation of a person's character (see p. 78)?

Pondering the Principles

1. Read 1 Corinthians 7:17-24, Philippians 4:11-12, 1 Timothy 6:6-8,

and Hebrews 13:5. Have you learned how to be content in any situation? Contentment is an important attitude to develop because when you have mastered it, you don't have to be controlled by your situation. God is not saying that we cannot work toward bettering our current situation (cf. 1 Cor. 7:21). However, it is important that we always keep our relationship to Christ as life's most important objective (Phil. 3:8) and that we do not become "servants of men" (1 Cor. 7:23) in pursuit of the passing material things of this temporal world (1 Tim. 6:7-8). We need to be free from the anxiety that discontentment brings (1 Cor. 7:21), realizing that God will provide the necessary grace in any situation so that we can concentrate on serving Him (2 Cor. 9:8-10).

2. Walking by the Spirit is achieved when we pattern our lives after Jesus Christ. Paul said, "Let the word of Christ dwell in you richly" (Col. 3:16). John said, "The one who says he abides in [Christ] ought himself to walk in the same manner as He walked" (1 John 2:6, NASB). How are you currently letting the Word dwell within you? Are you responding the way Christ would in each situation? The more familiar you become with the life of Christ by studying His life and His desires for your life, the more you will be led by the Spirit in becoming more like Christ.

3. Many people in society blame their problems on their environment. It's always much easier to blame someone or something else for your problems than to humbly admit you were wrong (cf. Gen. 3:11-13). Notice David's confession in Psalm 51:2-4. Are you quick to confess your sin to God and those you have wronged, or do you let pride prevent you from being spiritually cleansed? Being responsible for our actions is not a very popular concept, but we must recognize that the wickedness of our hearts (Jer. 17:9) is the source of our spiritual and sociological problems. Understanding that will make us more effective witnesses for Christ because we can focus on the cause of man's problems: sin.

6
Walking by the Spirit—Part 3

Outline

Introduction
A. The Impossible Standard
    1. God's expectation
    2. God's enablement
B. The Formidable Foe
C. The Sinful Flesh
    1. The problem
    2. The solution

Review
  I. The Command
 II. The Conflict
III. The Contrast
    A. The Works of the Flesh

Lesson
B. The Fruit of the Spirit
    1. The principles explained
       a) The significance of singularity
       b) The character of the Christian
       c) The attitude behind the action
          (1) Action fruit
          (2) Attitude fruit
    2. The particulars examined
       a) Love
       b) Joy
       c) Peace
       d) Long-suffering
       e) Gentleness
       f) Goodness
       g) Faithfulness
       h) Meekness

i) Self-control
        3. The purpose eliminated
IV. The Conquest
        A. God's Part
        B. Man's Part

Introduction

The Christian cannot walk independently of the Holy Spirit. He cannot operate on his own energy and have success because the Christian life is directly dependent on the Spirit's work. There are three things that make walking by the Spirit necessary for fulfilling God's plan for the Christian.

A. The Impossible Standard

1. God's expectation

God's standard for the believer is so high that there is no way a Christian could ever meet it, humanly speaking. Jesus expressed that unattainable standard when he said, "Be ye, therefore, perfect, even as your Father, who is in heaven, is perfect" (Matt. 5:48). Because of the impossible requirement of God's standard, it can be fulfilled only when we walk by the Spirit.

a) John 13:34—"A new commandment I give unto you, that ye love one another; as I have loved you, that ye also love one another" (cf. John 15:12). Doesn't that sound impossible?

b) Ephesians 4:30-32—"Grieve not the Holy Spirit of God, by whom ye are sealed unto the day of redemption. Let all bitterness, and wrath, and anger, and clamor, and evil speaking, be put away from you, with all malice; and be ye kind one to another, tenderhearted, forgiving one another, even as God, for Christ's sake, hath forgiven you." The standard is to be like Jesus and forgive as God has forgiven us.

c) Ephesians 5:20—We are to be "giving thanks always for all things." Even that one thing is an impossible standard from the standpoint of our humanness.

d) 1 John 2:6—John makes it obvious how impossible God's standard is: "He that saith he abideth in [Christ] ought himself also to walk, even as he walked."

2. God's enablement

Being like Christ is an impossible standard. That's why the believer must walk by the Spirit. It would be impossible to attain that standard on his own. Second Corinthians 6:16 contains the following promise of God to operate in the lives of His people: "I will dwell in them, and walk in them." It is God who dwells in the believer, empowering him to accomplish the task of walking by the Spirit. Walking by the Spirit is required because of the impossible standard God has set. It is attainable only by God Himself. Therefore, as you walk in Him, God's high standards are fulfilled in you.

B. The Formidable Foe

We could never fight Satan in our own strength. Keep in mind that the spiritual battle going on in the universe isn't primarily between Satan and Christians; it is between Satan and God. But we get in the middle of it. When people become "partakers of the divine nature" (2 Pet. 1:4) at the point of their salvation, they automatically find themselves in the middle of the battle. Because spiritual battles must be fought on a spiritual level, we must rely on divine resources to withstand the forces of Satan.

1. Ephesians 6:10, 12—"Finally, my brethren, be strong in the Lord, and in the power of His might. . . . For we wrestle not against flesh and blood, but against principalities, against powers, against the rulers of the darkness of this world, against spiritual wickedness in high places." Since we are flesh and blood, we cannot handle an enemy consisting of angelic beings outside our realm of combat. So we must be strong in the Lord.

2. James 4:7—Before we are told to resist the devil, James commands us to submit to God: "Submit yourselves, therefore, to God. Resist the devil, and he will flee from you." You must depend on God's power to resist Satan and his forces.

3. Jude 9—Even Michael, the champion angel, deferred to the superior power and authority of the Lord in a confrontation with Satan: "Michael, the archangel, when contending with the devil . . . dared not bring against him a railing accusation, but said, The Lord rebuke thee." Even Michael, who was the equal of Satan, did not rebuke him personally. It is clear to us then that because

of the formidable enemy we face, we cannot fight him with our own strength.

4. 1 John 4:4—"Greater is he that is in you, than he that is in the world." It's good to know that God's strength is always available.

C. The Sinful Flesh

1. The problem

We are all victimized by our own flesh. Romans 7 makes that clear. The apostle Paul delineates the conflict that takes place in every believer. Although he could say, "I delight in the law of God" (v. 22), he also said, "I know that in me (that is, in my flesh) dwelleth no good thing; for to will is present with me, but how to perform that which is good I find not. . . . But I see another law in my members, warring . . . and bringing me into captivity to the law of sin which is in my members. Oh, wretched man that I am!" (vv. 18, 23). Paul recognized he could not control his flesh in his own power.

2. The solution

The only way the flesh will ever be subdued becomes clear as we read Galatians 5:16: "Walk [by means of] the Spirit, and ye shall not fulfill the lust of the flesh." The only way you will ever conquer the flesh is by walking in the Spirit's power. You cannot conquer it by attempting to keep the law in your own strength. Because of God's impossible standard, our formidable foe, and our hopelessly sinful flesh we must walk by the Spirit. When you do that, the works of the flesh are not produced. Now let us consider the positive results of walking by the Spirit.

Review

I. THE COMMAND (v. 16; see pp. 52-54, 69-71)

II. THE CONFLICT (vv. 17-18; see pp. 54-63, 71-72)

III. THE CONTRAST (vv. 19-23; see pp. 73-78)

A. The Works of the Flesh (see vv. 19-21; see pp. 73-78)

Lesson

B. The Fruit of the Spirit (vv. 22-23)

"But the fruit of the Spirit is love, joy, peace, long-suffering, gentleness, goodness, faith, meekness, self-control; against such there is no law."

1. The principles explained

   a) The significance of singularity

   Notice that the "fruit" of verse 22 is singular in contrast to the "works" of verse 19, which is plural. The flesh manifests itself in many different ways, although not everyone practices all the works listed in verses 19-21. (No one could without destroying himself.) The Spirit, however, produces a single fruit, which signifies the unity of the spiritual qualities mentioned by Paul. When you walk by the Spirit, you will see not a few, but all facets of the fruit of the Spirit in your life. You either have all or none. That should produce a sense of relief because you don't need to run around and try to generate love or joy. You just need to walk by the Spirit and He will produce it all in you. God reduces everything to a common denominator—walking by the Spirit, which produces the fruit.

   b) The character of the Christian

   The fruit of the Spirit determines the character of the Christian. Each fruit forms the pattern that ought to be seen in the believer's life, although there will be times when we don't see them. When we fail to walk in the Spirit, we break the pattern. Whatever directs a person's heart determines what characterizes that person's life. In Mark 7, the disciples ask the Lord about a parable He had just given. He replied, "Are ye so without understanding also? Do ye not perceive, that whatsoever thing from outside entereth into the man, it cannot defile him; because it entereth not into his heart, but into the stomach, and goeth out into the draught [it is eliminated after the digestive process], purging all foods? And he said, That which cometh out of the man, that defileth the man. For from within, out of the heart of men, proceed evil thoughts, adulteries, fornications, murders, thefts, covetousness, wickedness, deceit, lasciviousness, an

85

evil eye, blasphemy, pride, foolishness. All these evil things come from within, and defile the man" (vv. 18-23). Christianity is not the philosophy of shaping up a person's environment to make him a better man, for it is man who contaminates the environment in the first place. A Christian's character is determined by the Spirit-led qualities that issue from his heart. Spiritual fruit is extremely important. It is the indicator that a man is saved. If there is no fruit in your life, something is wrong, because fruit is evidence that God is at work. God spoke through Hosea, saying, "From me is thy fruit found" (14:8). Whatever you do that is godly is from God. Walking in the Spirit produces fruit.

c) The attitude behind the action

(1) Action fruit

When you study the Bible, you will find that *fruit* means different things.

(a) Praise is "the fruit of our lips" (Heb. 13:15).

(b) Financial assistance to those in need is an example of fruit (Phil. 4:17).

(c) Praying with understanding is fruitful (1 Cor. 14:14).

(d) Godly deeds will be fruitful in the lives of those who "walk worthy of the Lord" (Col. 1:10).

(e) People won to Christ are "fruit unto life eternal" (John 4:36), and the first believers in Achaia were called "first fruits" (1 Cor. 16:15).

The Bible refers to different actions as being fruitful. But behind them are the necessary attitudes.

(2) Attitude fruit

Before you ever see the evidence of fruit, there must be a correct attitude, because attitudes produce actions. Whatever is going on inside a man will be manifested externally. The Christian life can be summarized by the attitudes of love, joy, peace, long-suffering, gentleness, goodness, faith, meekness, and self-control. If those attitudes are present, they will produce the appropriate actions. A Christian can't experience love or joy in a corner by himself because those are things that are shared with others. Fruit that is produced by the Spirit is not self-centered.

Is Your Fruit Basket Upside Down?

Christians are commanded to be fruitful, which requires depending on God. We can't be inactive and expect God to produce. We need to yield ourselves to God. The fruit of the Spirit in Galatians 5 is similar to the list of qualities in 2 Peter 1:5-7: "Add to your faith virtue; and to virtue knowledge; and to knowledge, self-control; and to self-control, patience; and to patience, godliness; and to godliness, brotherly kindness; and to brotherly kindness, love." Whereas Paul emphasized the divine source of those qualities, Peter emphasized the Christian's responsibility to acquire them. That is not a contradiction; it's the mysterious paradox of the Christian life—we are responsible to utilize God's power. Let me illustrate it this way: Imagine someone's picking fruit on a tree and throwing it down for you to catch in a basket. If you have your basket upside down and you're not paying attention, the fruit is going to drop on the ground. The Christian's responsibility is to get his basket in the right spot to receive the fruit the Holy Spirit is producing. The Christian life involves submitting yourself to the Holy Spirit.

2. The particulars examined

Commentators have tried to organize the fruit of the Spirit into different categories. Some say the first three are for God, the next three are for men, and the last three are for yourself. However, none of the outlines I found fit in every detail. The list of spiritual fruit is probably not complete. The phrase "and the like" (v. 21) tells us that the list of the works of the flesh is incomplete; the phrase "against such [things] there is no law" (v. 23) may indicate that the list of the fruit of the Spirit is also incomplete.

a) Love

(1) Its meaning

(a) The supreme gift

First Corinthians 13:13 says, "And now abideth faith, hope, love, these three; but the greatest of these is love." Some commentators believe that the qualities listed in Galations 5:22-23 are different manifestations of love. Love is clearly a dominate factor in human experience.

(b) The fulfillment of the law

Romans 13:10 says that a man who loves is fulfilling the law. Love is the basis of the church age. Galatians 5:14 says, "All the law is fulfilled in one word, even in this: Thou shalt love thy neighbor as thyself."

(c) The epitome of self-sacrifice

Love is not an emotion. It is an act of self-sacrifice. It is not necessarily feeling loving toward a particular person. It may not have any emotion connected with it. Romans 5:8 does not say, "God proved his love toward us in that while we were yet sinners, Christ had a warm feeling toward us." Rather, while we were sinners, "Christ died for us." Jesus said, "Greater love hath no man than this, that a man lay down his life for his friends" (John 15:13). God always defines biblical love in terms of self-sacrifice.

(d) The evidence of salvation

First John 3:14 says, "We know that we have passed from death unto life, because we love the brethren." Verse 17 says that since true love is expressed by meeting the needs of others, if you don't see that kind of love in your life, there is reason to question your salvation. Another reason for questioning your salvation is if you have misdirected love. First John 2:15 says, "Love not the world, neither the things that are in the world. If any man love the world, the love of the Father is not in him." If you are a new creation in Christ and the Spirit dwells within you and is producing fruit, love will be the pattern of your life. It will be broken by sin, but it will still be the general trend of your life.

(2) Its example

The supreme example of love is Jesus Christ Himself. In John 11 Jesus has arrived in Bethany at the request of Mary and Martha, the sisters of Lazarus, who is dead. John 11:33 says, "When Jesus, therefore, saw [Mary] weeping, and the Jews also weeping who came with her, he groaned in the spirit, and was troubled." When Jesus came to the tomb of Lazarus, He groaned and even wept. However, that wasn't because Lazarus was dead. In ten minutes Christ was going to raise him from the dead. In fact, He had purposely allowed Lazarus to die so He could display His glory by raising him. Jesus was crying about the consequences of sin—it brings death and creates sorrow. Verses 35-36 say, "Jesus wept. Then said the Jews, Behold how he loved him!" Jesus wept because He saw the power of sin in the life of someone He cared for.

(3) Its command

Before He died Himself, Jesus taught about the sacrificial nature of love, saying, "Greater love hath no man than this, that a man lay down his life for his friends" (John 15:13). Do you know you are commanded to love like that? Ephesians 5:1-2 says, "Be ye, therefore, followers of God, as dear children; and walk in love, as Christ hath also loved us."

(4) Its source

If you would like to love like that, let the Spirit produce it in you. Romans 5:5 says, "The love of God is shed abroad in our hearts by the Holy Spirit who is given unto us." The only way you'll ever see that kind of love generated in your life is through the Holy Spirit, the source and power of spiritual life.

b) Joy

(1) Its meaning

The word translated "joy" (Gk., *chara*) refers to the joy of God passing through a Christian. It is not just human joy that happens to be stimulated by divine influence. Nehemiah 8:10 says, "The

89

joy of the Lord is your strength." *Chara* is always used to refer to joy that is based on spiritual or religious factors. It is not a slaphappy silliness that is the result of positive circumstances, but the deep-founded joy of God. First Peter 1:8 says, "Whom, having not seen, ye love; in whom, though now ye see [Christ] not, yet believing, ye rejoice with joy unspeakable and full of glory." Spiritual joy transcends circumstances. In John 16:20, Jesus informs His disciples that they will weep and be sorrowful but that their sorrow will "be turned into joy." He illustrated the overriding power of joy with the example of childbirth: a woman has pain and apprehension in giving birth to a child, but that same incident also brings joy when the child is born (v. 21).

Divine joy is full joy. You can't add to it. First John 1:4 says, "These things write we unto you, that your joy may be full." Jesus makes a similar promise in John 16:24: "Hitherto have ye asked nothing in my name; ask, and ye shall receive, that your joy may be full." Our relationship to God brings joy and satisfaction.

(2) Its example

The greatest example of joy is Jesus. Although Isaiah 53:3 says that Jesus was "a man of sorrows, and acquainted with grief," Hebrews 12:2 says that Christ endured the cross "for the joy that was set before him." Jesus had so much joy that it didn't deter Him from paying the penalty for the sins of everyone who ever lived. He never lost the overriding joy in His life while anticipating the cross. And He can offer that kind of satisfying joy to His followers (John 15:11).

(3) Its command

Philippians 4:4 says, "Rejoice in the Lord always; and again I say, Rejoice."

(4) Its source

You say, "I would like to rejoice. How can I do it?" You don't try to do so on your own because the Holy Spirit produces it. Romans 14:17 says, "The kingdom of God is not food and drink, but righteousness, and peace, and joy in the Holy Spirit."

c) Peace

(1) Its meaning

The peace (Gk., *eirēnē*) spoken of here is a tranquility of mind based on a right relationship with God. It has nothing to do with circumstances. The verb form means "to bind together." You experience peace when nothing ruffles you because you know everything is under control. No matter what happens, you know that everything between you and God is right. When you remember that everything God is doing in your life is for your good (Rom. 8:28), that produces peace. Jesus said, "Let not your heart be troubled, neither let it be afraid" (John 14:27). Spiritual peace doesn't necessarily involve peaceful circumstances. However, if you carry a peaceful heart into turbulent circumstances, you'll still experience peace.

(2) Its example

The greatest example of peace is Jesus Christ, the Prince of Peace. Confidence in God and His promises supplied peace to Christ in the midst of temptation (Matt. 4:1-11). Jesus knew the Father would supply all He needed. The temptation He faced posed no threat to Him because He was convinced of the Father's care. Philippians 4:9 says, "Those things which ye have both learned, and received, and heard, and seen in me, do, and the God of peace shall be with you." If that's true, then verse 7 will be true: "The peace of God, which passeth all understanding, shall keep your hearts and minds through Christ Jesus." If the God of peace is with you, you will experience the peace of God. Certainly Jesus Christ had a tremendous sense of calm knowing God was there and working in His behalf.

(3) The command

Philippians 4:6 says, "Be anxious for nothing."

(4) Its source

Although we are commanded to be at peace, it is only the Holy Spirit that can produce peace, as Romans 14:17 indicates: "The kingdom of God is not food and drink, but righteousness, and peace, and joy in the Holy Spirit."

There's a paradox in the Christian life: Although we are commanded to exhibit spiritual fruit, it can never be produced except by yielding to the Holy Spirit.

d) Long-suffering

(1) Its meaning

Long-suffering means "patience," "tolerance," or "being slow to wrath." It is the opposite of impatience. The Bible reveals it as a characteristic of God in verses such as Psalm 86:15: "Thou, O Lord, art a God full of compassion, and gracious, long-suffering, and plenteous in mercy and truth." Unfortunately the word *long-suffering* sounds like merely being able to endure pain for a long time. But it really means being patient.

(2) Its example

Romans 2:4 tells us that God is patient, even though there are those who disregard His patience. Second Peter 3 records that some people were saying that Christ hadn't yet fulfilled the promise of His coming, and life would continue on as before. But Peter said that the only reason the Lord hasn't come in judgment is that He is "long-suffering toward us, not willing that any should perish" (v. 9). First Peter 3:20 speaks of the long-suffering of God in the days of Noah before He brought the Flood upon that ancient civilization. God's patience is always connected with mercy and should be reflected in the life of a Christian.

The supreme example of patience is Christ. Con sider how patient He was through all the things He endured in His ministry. In 1 Timothy 1:16 Paul speaks of Christ's example of patience: "For this cause I obtained mercy, that in me first Jesus Christ might show forth all long-suffering, for a pattern to them who should hereafter believe on him to life everlasting." In great patience the

Lord Jesus waited while Paul spent a portion of his adult life persecuting Christians. But Christ eventually redeemed him to make the apostle a prime example of His patience.

(3) Its command

There are several passages that command Christians to be patient. Colossians 3:12 says, "Put on, therefore, as the elect of God, holy and beloved, tender mercies, kindness, humbleness of mind, meekness, long-suffering" (Gk., *makrothumeō*, 'patience'; cf., Eph. 4:2-3; 2 Tim. 4:2).

(4) Its source

The source of patience is the Holy Spirit. Ephesians 3:16 tells us that Christians are "strengthened with might by [the] Spirit in the inner man." Paul prayed that the Colossians would be "strengthened with all might . . . unto all patience and long-suffering" (1:11).

e) Gentleness

(1) Its meaning

Gentleness means "tenderness." It is a characteristic of God and does not imply weakness. David says of God in 2 Samuel 22:36, "Thy gentleness hath made me great." It was also a characteristic of the apostle Paul. He told the Thessalonians, "We were gentle among you" (1 Thess. 2:7). Such gentleness, however, is not lacking in conviction. It allows for indignation when appropriate.

(2) Its example

Second Corinthians 10:1 says, "Now I, Paul, myself beseech you by the meekness and gentleness of Christ." Paul saw tremendous gentleness in Jesus. Christ's gentleness was demonstrated when He picked up little children, blessed them, and said, "Permit the little children to come unto me, and forbid them not" (Mark 10:14). Jesus also expressed gentleness when He said, "Take my yoke upon you, and learn of me; for I am meek and lowly in heart, and ye shall find rest unto your souls" (Matt. 11:29).

(3) Its command

We are commanded to be gentle. Second Timothy 2:24 says, "The servant of the Lord must not strive, but be gentle unto all men."

(4) Its source

James 3:17 implies that gentleness comes from the Holy Spirit. It says, "The wisdom that is from above is first pure, then peaceable, [and] gentle." Gentleness comes from God through the Holy Spirit.

f) Goodness

(1) Its meaning

Goodness refers to moral or spiritual excellence. God is good. Psalm 33:5 says, "The earth is full of the goodness of the Lord." Nehemiah 9 talks about His "great goodness" (vv. 25, 35). David anticipated that God's "goodness and mercy" would be with him throughout his life (Ps. 23:6). In Psalm 27:13 David says, "I had fainted unless I had believed to see the goodness of the Lord in the land of the living."

(2) Its example

The goodness of God is further exemplified in the life of Christ. When a rich young ruler came to Him and called Him "Good Master" (Mark 10:17), He said to him, "Why callest thou me good? There is none good but . . . God" (v. 18). Christ was assuming the character of God.

(3) Its command

We are commanded to be good in Galatians 6:10: "As we have, therefore, opportunity, let us do good unto all men, especially unto them who are of the household of faith."

(4) Its source and power

Although we are commanded to be good, that quality is produced by the Spirit. We cannot produce goodness on our own because in our own flesh "dwelleth no good thing" (Rom. 7:18). However, in 2 Thessalonians 1:11, we are told that God will "fulfill all the good pleasure of his goodness" in us.

g) Faithfulness

(1) Its meaning

Faithfulness means "trustworthiness, loyalty, or steadfastness." God is faithful. Lamentations 3:22-23 says, "It is because of the Lord's mercies that we are not consumed, because his compassions fail not. They are new every morning; great is thy faithfulness."

(2) Its example

As God in human flesh, Christ is to be trusted for His faithfulness. When He ascended to heaven, angels told the disciples, "This same Jesus . . . shall so come in like manner as ye have seen him go into heaven" (Acts 1:11). Do you think He will keep His promise? Revelation 19 reveals Christ returning to earth on a white horse, identified as "Faithful and True" (v. 11). He will keep His word.

(3) Its command

First Corinthians 4:2 says, "It is required in stewards, that a man be found faithful."

(4) Its source

Only the Holy Spirit can produce faithfulness in you. In Acts 6:5, the church in Jerusalem chooses Stephen, "a man full of faith and of the Holy Spirit," to administrate care for the widows in the church. Those two qualities go together.

h) Meekness

(1) Its meaning

Meekness is the only quality in the list that is not characteristic of God's essence. No Old Testament Scripture reveals God as meek. To be meek is to be lowly or humble. Obviously God is neither lowly or humble because of who He is. In the New Testament, meekness is described by three attitudes:

(*a*) Submissiveness to the will of God (James 1:21)

(*b*) Teachability (James 1:21)

(*c*) Consideration (1 Pet. 3:15)

(2) Its example

Second Corinthians 10:1 states that Jesus was meek. (His meekness was a manifestation of His humanity.) In Matthew 21:5, He rode into Jerusalem "meek, and sitting upon an ass."

(3) Its command

First Timothy 6:11 says, "Follow after . . . meekness." Colossians 3:12 says, "Put on . . . meekness."

(4) Its source

Only the Holy Spirit can produce meekness. Galatians 5:23 tells us meekness is the fruit of the Spirit.

i) Self-control

(1) Its meaning

Self-control is the ability to keep one's self in check.

(2) Its example

Hebrews 13:8 says, "Jesus Christ, the same yesterday, and today, and forever."

(3) The command

Peter exhorts us to add self-control to our knowledge (2 Pet. 1:6).

(4) Its source

Self-control is produced only by the Holy Spirit.

All of the fruit of the Spirit is commanded of the believer, produced by the Holy Spirit, and exemplified by Jesus Christ.

3. The purpose eliminated

Paul ends his listing of the fruit of the Spirit with this statement: "Against such there is no law" (v. 23). He is saying that if you're in the Spirit, you don't need the law, which had one purpose: restraining sin. As the flesh produced evil, the law helped to restrain it. In the case of the Christian, the law is unnecessary because the Spirit more effectively restrains the works of the flesh.

IV. THE CONQUEST (vv. 24-25)

A. God's Part (v. 24)

"And they that are Christ's have crucified the flesh with the affections and lusts."

If you are a Christian, your flesh was crucified the moment you believed in Jesus Christ. It's a dead issue. Paul said in Galatians 2:20, "I am crucified with Christ." Your old life is gone. God crucified your sinful nature with its passions and desires on the cross.

B. Man's Part (v. 25)

"If we live [by] the Spirit, let us also walk [by] the Spirit."

Since God has paid the penalty for our sinfulness, we ought to be consistent in living the life He has enabled us to live.

Focusing on the Facts

1. Because of the impossible standard that God requires, what is the only way a Christian can fulfill God's plan for him (see p. 82)?
2. Who is the spiritual battle in the universe primarily between (see p. 83)?
3. Why must Christians rely on divine resources to withstand the forces of Satan (see p. 83)?
4. What does James 4:7 tell believers they must do before resisting the devil (see p. 83)?
5. When a Christian walks by the Spirit, will he manifest all the fruit of the Spirit? Explain (see p. 85).
6. What does spiritual fruit indicate (see p. 85)?
7. What are some examples of action fruit in the New Testament (see p. 86)?
8. What paradox of the Christian life is seen by comparing Galatians 5:22-23 with 2 Peter 1:5-7 (see p. 87)?
9. Describe the character of biblical love (see p. 88).
10. Of what is the expression of Christian love evidence in 1 John? What are two things that could rightfully lead a person to question his salvation (see p. 88)?
11. How did Jesus demonstrate the greatness of His love, as implied in John 15:13 (see p. 89)?
12. Why was Jesus not deterred from paying the penalty for the sins of mankind (Heb. 12:2; see p. 90)?
13. What is the biblical definition of peace (see p. 91)?
14. What supplied peace to Christ in the midst of temptation (see p. 91)?
15. How is God patient toward mankind, according to 2 Peter 3:9?

What other divine attribute is connected to God's patience (see p. 92)?

16. Why did Christ patiently show mercy toward Paul while he was persecuting the church (1 Tim. 1:16; see pp. 92-93)?

17. Does gentleness lack in conviction? What does it allow for (see p. 93)?

18. What does Paul command "the servant of the Lord" to be like toward "all men" in 2 Timothy 2:24 (see p. 94)?

19. How did the angels at Christ's ascension imply that He would be faithful (Acts 1:11; see p. 95)?

20. What is the one spiritual fruit that is not an attribute of God (see p. 95)?

21. What three attitudes are descriptive of meekness (see p. 96)?

22. Why is the Mosaic law unnecessary for the Christian (see p. 97)?

23. Explain the cooperation between man and God in conquering the flesh (see p. 97).

Pondering the Principles

1. Have you recognized the impossibility of living the Christian life apart the Holy Spirit? Maybe you have never realized all that the Spirit does for you. Match the following verses with the appropriate ministries of the Spirit in the life of a believer:

a. He bestows spiritual gifts.	John 16:12-15
b. He guarantees the believer's glorification.	Romans 8:26-27
c. He teaches us.	Galatians 5:22-23
d. He guides us.	Acts 1:8
e. He prays for us.	Ephesians 1:13-14
f. He fights the flesh.	Acts 16:6-7, 10
g. He produces spiritual fruit.	Galatians 5:17
h. He sanctifies us.	2 Thessalonians 2:13
i. He empowers us for service.	Romans 8:16
j. He provides assurance of salvation.	Romans 12:3-8

Praise God for the Holy Spirit enabling you to live a life that is "acceptable unto the Lord" (Eph. 5:10).

2. Galatians 6:10 says, "As we have opportunity, let us do good to all people, especially to those who belong to the family of believers" (NIV). How would you rate your desire to help others? Do you look for opportunities to help your neighbors, friends, and relatives who don't know Christ? Or do you avoid interacting with them? If so, why? Did another Christian's good works and character lead you to Christ, causing you to glorify Him

(Matt. 5:16)? Commit yourself to doing good deeds as a foundation for evangelism. Futhermore, assuming you are a member of a local church, make sure you are actively involved and available to do good to that family of believers.

3. Read in Luke 4:1-13 how Jesus exhibited self-control. Who was Jesus being led by (v. 1)? What demonstrates that Jesus' desire was not self-gratification? Whose authority did He submit to (vv. 8, 12)? Although He was victorious over Satan's attack, did that mean victory was complete (v. 13)? Self-control is a spiritual quality that often alludes us. Do you find it easy to do what you want to do and disregard God's will? When faced with a situation that demands self-control, always consider how God would have you respond and ask Him to enable you to follow the Spirit's leading. Our life's motto should be, "Not my will, but yours be done" (Luke 22:42, NIV).

Scripture Index

Exodus
20:13 — 12
20:15 — 12
21:1-6 — 35-46

Leviticus
19:18 — 43

2 Samuel
22:36 — 91

Nehemiah
8:10 — 87
9:25, 35 — 92

Psalms
23:6 — 92
27:13 — 92
33:5 — 92
86:15 — 90

Isaiah
53:3 — 88

Lamentaions
3:22-23 — 93

Hosea
14:8 — 84

Jonah
4:7 — 22

Matthew
4:1-11 — 89
5:28 — 76
5:48 — 80
8:11-12 — 7
11:29 — 91-92
18:1-6 — 25
21:5 — 94
23:33 — 24

Mark
7:15 — 76
7:18-23 — 84
7:20-23 — 71
10:14 — 91
10:17-18 — 92

Luke
18:9-14 — 29
24:39 — 52

John
4:34 — 38
8:31 — 23
8:34 — 33
8:36 — 33
10:28-29 — 23
11:33, 35-36 — 87
13:34 — 80
14:16 — 69
14:27 — 89
15:4-8 — 23
15:11 — 88
15:13 — 86-87
16:13 — 60
16:14 — 60
16:20-21 — 88
16:24 — 88

Acts
1:8 — 60
1:11 — 93
4:12 — 28

6:5	93	14:1-3	39-41
6:7	19	14:4-5	41
6:13	27	14:10	41
10:9-15	34	14:13	41-42
10:13-15	40	14:14-15	42
16:1-3	25	14:17	88-90
16:3	5	14:17, 20	42
		14:21	42
Romans		15:1-3	43
2:4	90	15:3	38
2:8	19-20	15:18	20
4:1	53	15:32	3
5:1-2	67	16:26	20
5:5	44, 87		
5:8	86	**1 Corinthians**	
6:12-13	56-57	4:2	93
6:16-18	20	5:1	72
6:17	20	5:6	22
6:19	53	6:13, 18	72
7:5	53	6:19	67
7:8-10	59	7:1-2	72
7:12	17	7:17	64
7:13	70	8:4	12
7:14-19, 21-25	54	8:8	12
7:18	53, 93	9:20-22	26
7:18, 22-23	82	9:27	57-58
7:22	43	13:13	85-86
8:3	55	14:14	84
8:4	13	15:56	59
8:9	51, 69	16:15	84
8:9-11	37		
8:12-13	57	**2 Corinthians**	
8:14	60	5:7	65
8:16	60	5:17	52
8:19, 21	10	6:16	81
8:26	55	9:8	9
8:28	89	10:1	91, 94
8:30	22	10:4-5	20
9:30-32	7		
10:16	20	**Galatians**	
11:6	6	1:13-14	27
13:8-9	13	2:20	52, 58, 95
13:9-10	44	3:3	53
13:10	86	3:10	8
13:13	64	3:13	3
13:13-14	44-56	3:25-26	4
13:14	38	4:6	4
		4:10	6

4:10-11	34
5:1	4, 17, 33, 60
5:1-12	5, 18
5:2	5-7, 9
5:2-4	6
5:2-6	5, 18
5:3	7-8
5:4	8-10
5:5	2, 10-11
5:6	11-13
5:7	18-21
5:7-12	5
5:8	21-22
5:9	22-23
5:10	23-25
5:11	25-28
5:12	28
5:13	33-43
5:13-15	49
5:13-16	35
5:14	13, 43-44, 86
5:15	43
5:16	2, 44-45, 49-52, 58, 60, 67-69, 82
5:16-18	48
5:16-25	49, 64
5:17	52-58
5:18	2, 58-61
5:18, 25	49
5:19, 22	83
5:19-21	71-75, 83
5:21	75-76, 85
5:22-23	3, 48, 60, 71, 83-95
5:23	85, 94
5:24	95
5:25	2, 95
6:2	3
6:10	92
6:12	53
6:12-13	19

Ephesians

1:6	33
1:11	91
2:14	35
2:18	60
3:16	49, 91
4:2-3	64, 91
4:17-23	65-66
4:30-32	80
5:1-2	87
5:2-3	66
5:3	73
5:8	66
5:15-16	66-67
5:17	70
5:18	49, 70
5:18-21	61
5:18-22, 25	68
5:20	80
6:1, 4-5, 9	68
6:6	94
6:10, 12	81

Philippians

1:6	23
3:10	56
4:4	88
4:6	89
4:7, 9	89
4:17	84

Colossians

1:10	18, 65, 84
2:6	69
3:5	57
3:9	36
3:12	91, 94
3:16—4:1	68
4:5	67

1 Thessalonians

2:7	91
4:3	72

2 Thessalonians

1:8	20
1:11	93
2:13	60
2:13-14	22
3:6-7, 11	66

1 Timothy

1:16	90
4:1-2	21
4:4	40
6:11	94

2 Timothy

2:3-6	58
2:24	92
3:8	21
4:2	91

Hebrews

12:1	57
12:2	88
13:8	38, 94
13:15	84

James

1:21	94
2:10	8
3:17	92
4:7	81

1 Peter

1:8	88
1:22	21
2:16	41
3:15	94
3:20	90

2 Peter

1:4	81

1:5-7	85
1:6	94
2:1-2	21
2:1-14	24
2:18-19	37
3:9	90
3:18	9

1 John

1:4	88
2:6	80
2:15	86
3:2	10
3:14, 17	86
4:4	82

3 John

3-4	67

Jude

4	37
9	81
11-13	22

Revelation

9:21	74
19:11	93

Moody Press, a ministry of the Moody Bible Institute, is designed for education, evangelization, and edification. If we may assist you in knowing more about Christ and the Christian life, please write us without obligation: Moody Press, c/o MLM, Chicago, Illinois 60610.